THE
HELL
YOU NEVER
KNEW

and How to Avoid
Going There

RYUHO OKAWA

IRH PRESS

BOOKS
IRH PRESS
New York

Library of Congress Cataloging-in-Publication Data

ISBN 13: 978-1-942125-52-5
ISBN 10: 1-942125-52-6

Printed in Canada

First Edition

Cover Design: Whitney Cookman

Contents

CHAPTER TWO

An Exploration into the World of Hell

A Tour of Modern Hell Experienced During Sleep

4. The Hell of Hungry Ghosts: Food is Taken Away

5. The Middle Way of Life: How to Avoid Hell

Further Readings: Self-reflection will lead you up

CHAPTER THREE

Seeking the Starting Point of Enlightenment

Three Checkpoints to Determine Heaven or Hell

1. The Starting Point of Enlightenment (1): The Awareness that Humans are Spiritual Beings

2. The Starting Point of Enlightenment (2): The Way You Live Determines Your Destination in the Afterlife

PREFACE

I would like for each and every one of you to have this book so you can read and reread anytime. People with a short time left should study this book as a must-read. Bereaved families who have held funeral services should also study this book, for their understanding of its contents will serve to console the souls of the deceased and bring them salvation.

People have created a new hierarchical social system in this world, which is based on academic achievements, physical appearance, status, assets, or name recognition of the company where one works. However, heaven and hell absolutely do exist, transcending all of this. Even if there may be no problem for those who can return to heaven, the truth of the matter is that about half of the people living today are headed for hell.

This stands to reason; today's leaders that are of the intellectual class believe that atheism and materialism are Truth. Even those in religious positions such as clerics of Buddhist temples and Shinto shrines have allowed themselves to be brainwashed to believe that only that which is taught in school is correct and scientific, because they do not want to be thought of as primitives.

With the *Bon* season* approaching, now is the perfect time to read this book and dedicate it to your ancestors.

Ryuho Okawa
Founder and CEO
Happy Science Group

---

* According to the Buddhist tradition, the Bon season is a period usually in mid-July in the modern calendar or in mid-August in the lunar calendar, and it is believed that even the gates of hell opens for a week or so. People in Buddhist countries generally believe that spirits in the other world come and visit their offspring during this season so they offer various things on the altar at home, including incense, flowers, and the ancestors' favorite food, as a way of comforting these spirits.

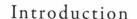

The Modern Hell:
A Possible Outcome
For Anyone

Introduction

The Modern Hell:
A Possible Outcome for Anyone

More than half of people today are headed to hell

While I don't know the exact number of people who die each year, if we suppose it is one million, over five hundred thousand people, undoubtedly, go to the world known as hell. Some have already gone and others are going in that direction at this very moment. Every year, as you read books and enjoy a relaxed life, hundreds of thousands of people are headed to the underworld.

People tend to think of hell as an imagined concept that appears in ancient Buddhism or old myths to instruct people through fear. But the truth is that there is a hell. The different realms of hell taught in Buddhism actually do exist exactly the way they are described.

I see those suffering in hell every day—day after day. It is pitiful. It is painful to see those who hardly look human anymore. When they were alive, they were ordinary people just like everybody else, wearing business attire, holding certain social positions and making a regular living. However, once people die and leave their physical bodies upon returning to the other world, their minds become what they are. People who had always harbored negative thoughts would unfortunately transform in the way that most shows the characteristics of their thoughts.

However beautiful a woman may have been, if she lived in a wrong way filled with malicious thoughts, she will turn ugly all at once when she no longer has a physical body, because no matter how hard she may pretend to be good, what is in her mind will be her outward manifestation in the other world. On the contrary, a woman who was not blessed with good looks but lived rightly filled with faith in God and love for others will start manifesting the true nature of her soul after death, transforming into a beautiful figure emanating divine light. The same goes for men. In the end, people will go to a place that corresponds to their own state of mind after they die.

Hell is only a small part of the vast spirit world

From ancient times, people have wondered why hell should exist and why God leaves it untouched. It may be a natural question for people to ask, especially if they are already in hell or near it. But in fact, if we compare the size of the spirit world to a fifty-story building, hell is only the size of the basement. The building may have five basement floors, but there are fifty stories above the ground. This is the basic structure of the spirit world; it predominantly consists of heaven, and hell is only the small part below ground.

The fact that the underground part exists shows that there is a passing mark for our spiritual training as children of God and that some people cannot make it. Not everybody can get a perfect score, and not everybody can pass. Those who live in a selfish and egotistical way will face consequences. There is a certain passing mark that's necessary to enter heaven, and those who don't reach it will find themselves in hell.

There is a minimum standard that we, as children of God, need to meet to move up from hell to heaven. There is a certain way of life that we are expected to pursue in this world, and there will always be some who do not clear this minimum requirement.

The common trait of those who go to hell

Heaven is made up of worlds on different levels. Just as students are placed in different classes based on the results of their placement tests, spirits in heaven are divided into separate groups and reside on different levels layered on top of one another. In this world, placement tests measure students' academic abilities, but in heaven, it is the level of spirits' faith that determines which level of heaven they

The Dimensional Structure of the Other World

Ninth Dimension – The Cosmic Realm:
The realm of the saviors

Eighth Dimension – The Realm of Tathagatas:
The realm of spirits who were central figures in shaping the history of particular eras

Seventh Dimension – The Realm of Bodhisattvas:
The realm of spirits whose main focus is on helping others

Sixth Dimension – The Realm of Light:
The realm of specialists and divine spirits

Fifth Dimension – The Realm of Goodness:
The realm of good-hearted spirits

Fourth Dimension – The Posthumous Realm:
The realm where people go immediately after death

Hell

Hell is much smaller than heaven; it exists in the lower part of the Posthumous Realm.

Third Dimension – Earthly Realm

should reside in. Spirits in heaven are ranked solely based on their level of faith.

The spirit world consists of different dimensions, from the fourth to the fifth, sixth, and beyond. Each of these dimensions is divided into about three levels, which are further broken down into smaller groups. The spirits in heaven belong to different groups depending on their level of faith.

Hell is essentially a world inhabited by those who do not have religious faith, namely those who hold mistaken beliefs, atheists, and materialists. In addition to those who didn't believe in God, there are hypocrites who acted like they had faith while they were alive, but didn't really believe in their hearts. Those who went to church every Sunday only for the sake of appearances and did not actually believe will also find themselves in hell after they die.

Even temples and churches exist in hell; priests, ministers, and monks who held and taught mistaken beliefs while they were alive engage themselves in religious activities in the shallow parts of hell. In these religious facilities, they give sermons, but there is something wrong with what they are teaching. The hypocrites assemble and listen to these sermons, believing they are leading religious lives, but these people haven't realized the mistakes in their religious beliefs.

What happens to those who have fallen to hell? (1)
— The cases of doctors, nurses, and judges

There are various ways to measure our status in this world; for instance, social position, income, and academic background. But these worldly factors are irrelevant to whether we go up to heaven or go down to hell, because our destination will be determined based on a completely different set of values.

A typical image of hell that Japanese people had back in the Heian period (794 – 1192) was that it was a place where ogres chased the dead, boiled them in a bubbling cauldron, roasted them over a fire, and ate them. These ogres would also shatter people's skulls with clubs.

Today, these ogres have been replaced by evil-hearted surgeons, nurses, public prosecutors, judges, and members of the press (although, of course, the majority of people in these professions are good people). In the hospitals of hell, vicious surgeons with mouths torn to their ears kill their "patients" by slicing them up with scalpels, hiding their malevolent grins behind surgical masks. And the victims go through the endless cycle of being killed and coming back to life.

There are also nurses in hell. Those who worked as nurses but lacked a heart of love when they were alive help the surgeons by kidnapping, incarcerating, and killing their patients. Wicked public prosecutors arrest the dead and find pleasure in tormenting them. Evil police officers also take the place of ogres.

A Japanese folktale tells a story about the king of hell, Enma, who is said to be a judge of the afterlife. In fact, judges in the world after death today wear black robes just as they do here. There are judges in heaven as well as in hell—they're people who like sitting in judgment on others.

Judges who hand out wrong judgments that go against their own consciences while they are alive end up in hell. These people stand in judgment over the dead, writing up and reading out death sentences such as "this person is sentenced to be torn limb from limb." Regardless of our social status or occupation here on Earth, we are divided into two opposite destinations in the afterlife.

Doctors exist not only in hell but also in heaven. Surgeons in heaven remove the malignant parts of the spiritual bodies of the souls who have just moved up from hell. They perform operations to remove the part of the astral body that is negatively affected by the persons mental condition. Nurses in heaven help new arrivals from hell as they undergo rehabilitation. Judges in heaven use the right perspective on life to determine the appropriate destination for each soul.

What happens to those who have fallen to hell? (2)
— The case of reporters

Members of the press who acted on their consciences with an earnest wish to right evil and improve the world write articles for newspapers or broadcast news about events in heaven. There are all types of people that take part in a variety of activities in the spirit world.

We can also find newspaper reporters in hell. These reporters reside in the upper reaches of hell, writing articles for the newspapers published in hell. They write stories about recent arrivals to hell. If they find a newcomer who was a famous figure on Earth, they add a large headline like, "The President of Such-and-Such Company Arrives in Hell. Let's Beat Him Up!" They also write follow-up stories to keep readers informed. The headline to a follow-up story may read, "President Impeached and Torn Limb from Limb," "President Burned to Death," or "President Falls to a Lower Level of Hell," depending on what has happened to him.

It is one hundred percent true that hell exists

It is my earnest desire to prevent people from falling to hell. If more than half of the people who will die are headed to such a place, it is only natural that we, as fellow humans, should tell them of their mistakes in their ways of living and warn them of the danger of falling there. There is nothing worse than shutting one's eyes to people who are about to cross a busy street on a red light, or about to fall over a cliff. We cannot possibly ignore them without offering a helping hand.

Today, the number of those who actually go to hell is significant; many suffer in the underworld for decades, or hundreds of years after they die. Knowing the Truth and abiding by it while alive will help them evade such agony. This is what it means to preserve human dignity.

Hell is a world created by our own minds and is not a place for punishment or torture. In this material earthly world, things do not often go as we would wish but in the other world, our thoughts manifest instantly. The spirit world is such a place.

It is only natural for us, who live in the same environment as our fellow humans, to want to save others if we know suffering awaits them in the future. While it is up to each individual whether to believe me or not, the truth is the truth; I see and experience the spirit world every single day. For me there is no room for doubt; it is one hundred percent true that the other world exists.

What if today's atheists, who have no knowledge of the soul or the other world, end up in hell? How can they escape there? How can they be saved? The only way to escape hell is to enter the right path: correct your mind and strive to develop in the direction of God, or Buddha. There is no other way than this. To walk this path, having knowledge of the right rules is indispensable; otherwise, it is the same as being lost in a maze, unable to find a way out. That is why it is extremely important to learn the Truth while you are still alive.

Chapter One

Introduction to The World of Hell

A Report on the Six Realms of Hell,
Described by Princess Kozakura

Princess Kozakura:
A Respected 16th Century
Japanese Woman

Her spiritual message

A Collection of Spiritual Messages by Ryuho Okawa (Happy Science) contains the "Spiritual Message from Princess Kozakura—Part 1" in Vol. 26, the contents of which are quite understandable for beginners. I believe such introductory stories of the Divine Realms of the spirit world have significance as Happy Science continues to increase its number of new believers. Though the theme may be simple, they contain many important points, so I have decided to speak more in depth about them. In her spiritual message, Princess Kozakura covers a variety of topics, but here I will mainly focus on her descriptions of hell, namely, Chapter Two of Vol. 26, "The World of Hell and the World of *Ryugu* (literally, "dragon palace")."

Princess Kozakura lived in 16th century Japan.* I did not have any direct connection with her until I received spiritual messages from her. I first got to know about her while I was a lay person working in Nagoya

City some time ago. The employee dormitory of the company I worked for in Nagoya at the time is now a Happy Science facility renamed Nagoya Kinen-kan (Nagoya Commemoration Hall). While I lived there, I started to publish spiritual message books, which gradually began to appear in bookstores. So I would often visit bookstores to see how they were selling, and one day I happened to find the book, *The Tale of Princess Kozakura—A Communication from the Spirit World*, one from the Wasaburo Asano Collections published by the same company that had published my books (Chobunsha). Reading this book, I first became familiar with Princess Kozakura.

The Tale of Princess Kozakura

While Wasaburo Asano (1874 – 1937) is now fading from modern memory, he was quite famous before World War II. He was active in the heyday of the

---

[*] Princess Kozakura was the wife of Arajiro Yoshimitsu (also known as Yoshioki) Miura, a warlord in the late Muromachi Era (1336 – 1573). In 1516, as Yoshimitsu waged war against the army of Hojo Sou'un, he became besieged inside the Arai castle (located in Abura-tsubo, Miura City, Kanagawa Prefecture) with his father Dosun (Yoshiatsu). He was finally defeated, dying by his own sword, and this resulted in the downfall of the entire Miura Family. Princess Kozakura mourned her husband's death and continued to pray for the repose of the family's souls, but she eventually died from disease while still young. Her way of life deeply impressed the local people by her exemplary display of womanly virtues.

Oomoto-kyo religion* and afterward during the suppression of the religion. He was originally an English language teacher at the Naval Engineering College, one of the most prestigious schools in pre-War Japan. He graduated from the English Literature Department of the Tokyo Imperial University (now the University of Tokyo), which also produced renowned novelists such as Soseki Natsume and Ryunosuke Akutagawa.

During the growth period of Oomoto-kyo, guided by Onisaburo Deguchi, Asano visited the religious headquarters located in Ayabe, a city in Kyoto Prefecture. Later, he learned the spiritual training method "Chinkon Kishin" (calming the soul and attuning oneself to the divine) from Onisaburo Deguchi and started to experience different kinds of spiritual phenomena. This led him to develop a firm belief in Oomoto-kyo and he started to devote his time and energy to its activities; having resigned his teaching position, he began working primarily as an editor of the internal journal of Oomoto-kyo.

Being a graduate from the English Literature Department of the University of Tokyo and a translator of English books, Wasaburo Asano was regarded a highly

---

* Oomoto-kyo is a new Japanese religion. It was founded by Nao Deguchi in 1892, and was led by a spiritual teacher Onisaburo Deguchi. Nao Deguchi was inspired by a spirit which called itself, *Ushitora no Konjin* (literally, "God of Northeast"), and received messages called *Ofude-saki* (literally, "writings") which were automatic writings. The messages included an apocalyptic philosophy calling for social reform, which was deemed critical of the government as it would instigate revolution, thereby leading to government condemnation and suppression before World War II.

intellectual in those times. Thus, Oomoto-kyo was able to secure a person of intellectual stature as its representative. After Asano became a believer, more of the intellectual class started to join Oomoto-kyo, followed by many others who were involved in the military and the Imperial Household. Oomoto-kyo created sensational news in this way during that time.

After that, however, Oomoto-kyo was suppressed by the government and suffered a downturn. This led Wasaburo Asano to separate from Oomoto-kyo and start his own group; he published the magazine *Shinreikai* (literally, "Inner Spirit World") and, as the chief editor, investigated various psychic activities, serving to nurture and educate people about the many aspects of spiritual phenomena.

Although Wasaburo Asano himself did not possess spiritual power, his wife Takeko did; she had developed the ability to convey spiritual messages. *The Tale of Princess Kozakura—A Communication from the Spirit World* was the transcription and compilation of the spiritual messages his wife had channeled.*

Princess Kozakura was, in fact, Takeko's guardian spirit. She was the wife of a manorial warlord's son

---

* Takeko, the wife of Wasaburo Asano, started receiving spiritual messages from Shinju, her second son who had died suddenly in 1929. Eventually she started spiritual communication with Princess Kozakura, who revealed herself as Takeko's guardian spirit. Wasaburo took on the role of *saniwa*, a person who would judge the credibility of spiritual messages, and recorded the messages of Princess Kozakura, which were then published in 1937 as *The Tale of Princess Kozakura—A Communication from the Spirit World*. It created a large following of readers.

living in the 16th century. Although she was not known for any particularly great achievement, she was highly respected for the attitude she held; she apparently lived a pure-hearted life and served many people, a way of life that would be considered ideal for Japanese women. In homage to her virtue, there is even a shrine named after her, the Kozakura Hime Jinja (Princess Kozakura Shrine, in Miura City, Kanagawa Prefecture). I myself have never been there, but there is such a shrine. She was a person of reverence for a certain group of people.

The sixth dimension where Princess Kozakura resides

Where in the spirit world does Princess Kozakura actually reside? In terms of the multi-dimensional structure taught by Happy Science (see page 15, Introduction), she resides in the upper realm of the sixth dimension, which is home to various gods.

I have observed that the spiritual messages of the spirits in the sixth dimension are generally very concrete and detailed in content. These spirits are able to still clearly see humanly activities in this world as well as in the other world, and there is a high degree of detail in their explanations. They still retain human-like lifestyles in the sixth dimension, and their views of the spirit world are humanlike in character. That is why we can easily understand their messages. The spiritual messages from sixth-dimensional spirits such as Princess Kozakura and the 10th-century Japanese female novelist Murasaki Shikibu give us a very concrete and realistic image of the spirit world. Because of the detailed descriptions, we can understand the lifestyles of the sixth dimension and below.

On the other hand, the seventh-dimensional bodhisattvas and the eighth-dimensional tathagatas, who constitute the major part of Happy Science Guiding Spirit Group, tend to speak of ideological and abstract matters. In those realms of the spirit world, spirits do not retain a human lifestyle nor do they live like humans on Earth. So it is easy for us to imagine the lives of the spirits in the sixth dimension and below, while we can only have a vague image of the lives in the seventh-dimensional Realm of Bodhisattvas and above. These spirits no more have concrete lifestyle and they are only active as thought energy. For this reason, readers may probably find stories of the spirits that still retain a human image easier to understand than the high spirits' abstract messages.

The spiritual message from Princess Kozakura is mainly based on what was communicated to me through automatic writing, not channeled through me verbally, and in this sense, it is different from other selections in my Spiritual Messages Collection. From the content, I surmise that she had some kind of "tutor" to help her convey the messages. The contents of her message started out at a relatively low level, compared to the overall level of Happy Science teachings, but I had the impression that at a certain point, a "tutor" started to help her and had given her advice as she conveyed messages to me. Some bodhisattvas were probably instructing her behind the scenes, and she was telling me what she had learned in her own words and opinions, and acted like a "translator." This is the basic background of the Spiritual Message from Princess Kozakura.

There are many points I would like to cover, but here I will focus on what has been written about the world of hell in the Spiritual Message from Princess Kozakura, because her descriptions are quite concrete. It is notable that there are some new points presented here for the first time. Let me now begin the explanation of the various realms in the underworld Princess Kozakura observed.

2

The Hell of Villains:
Repeatedly Killing Each Other

The Hell of Villains, according to Princess Kozakura

Firstly, Princess Kozakura speaks on the Hell of Villains as follows:

Princess Kozakura: This is hell, but still a shallow part. The sky is dull and gray; it seems like it is dusk or before daybreak. The scenery is somewhat blurry, but still clear enough to recognize things.

I can see a river nearby. It gives off a rather foul smell, and I get an uneasy feeling. Sure enough, many dead human bodies lie in the shallow waters and there is even a corpse with a hand reaching out into the empty air. But once I get closer, the bodies I thought were corpses are actually writhing in the water; they are still alive.

As I observe this scene, I hear screams coming from the upper part of the river. I look up and see about twenty people chasing a couple, a man and woman, coming in my direction. The couple is then caught at the foot of a bridge and tied there with rope. Both the man and the woman are only wearing worn-out, mud-covered kimonos.

The man is bleeding from his forehead.

Suddenly, a booming voice is heard. It is from the largest man among the chasers. He is over three meters (10 feet) in height. His arms are immensely thick; maybe double the thickness of one of my thighs. His face illuminated by torchlight is exactly like that of red ogres we hear about in old stories, the only difference being that he has no horns. He even has what look like fangs sticking out of his mouth.

By command of the large man, five men start to sharpen their swords on the riverside. Their swords have large blades, like Chinese broadswords. They grind edges on these swords using whetstones, dipping and rinsing them in the river. The awful metallic sounds of grinding blades ring through the icy air.

The poor couple had actually been exploited like slaves by the red ogre. They run away, but only to be chased down and captured again. I will leave it to the imagination how the couple was then cut up with the broadswords and their bodies thrown into the river.

Apparently, this place is the Hell of Villains, which is governed by the fear of anything related to the harm of the physical body. It is a world of fear in which you never know when your life will be taken. In modern terms, you could call it the world of sadists and masochists.

The young couple who were killed in this case will continually get killed by the ogres until they realize that their lives are eternal and imperishable. In this sense, the ogres are their teachers. On the other hand, the ogres will kill the same person again and again until they begin to understand the meaninglessness of taking lives in anger. In this sense, the murdered couple also serve as teachers for the ogres. My visit to this Hell of Villains made me keenly aware that humans need to be free of fear to be happy.

The inhabitants will continue killing each other in this realm for two or three hundred years until they finally realize that humans are children of God and have eternal life. After getting weary of killing, some will awaken to the Truth and go up to heaven, while others will harden in their cruelty and fall into a deeper part of hell.

It is rare for the inhabitants to stay there for four or five hundred years; in most cases, as I just said, they will move on to their next phase after two to three hundred years. The opportunity to save these spirits comes at this turning point of after two or three hundred years, so we must take advantage of this timing. When they become tired of the slaughter and start to question their behavior, angels of light will come to persuade them of the Truth.

It seems that, to a certain extent, God values salvation through one's own effort even in this realm, and implements a system in which angels intervene for the first time when the inhabitants' hearts start to turn toward God.

Excerpt from Vol. 26, *A Collection of Spiritual Messages by Ryuho Okawa*

Still a shallow part of hell

Princess Kozakura says that the Hell of Villains is still in the shallow part of the underworld. According to her description, the sky is dull and gray, as if at dusk or before daybreak, and the scenery is slightly dimmed. The brightness of the sky around sundown or before daybreak where there is weak sunlight suggests that the heavenly world is relatively close. It means that the light of the spiritual sun in the spirit world still shines thinly through the clouds, although not directly. This is the level at which this hell is located.

The fourth dimensional world can be roughly divided into three parts. The first one is a place we call the Posthumous Realm. It is the place for the spirits who have just returned to the other world just after death and whose eventual destination has yet to be determined. This is the regular station, or middle area, of the fourth dimension. Above this is the Astral Realm, a somewhat more purified area of the fourth dimension. Below the Posthumous Realm, on the other hand, is the world of hell. The fourth dimension is the beginning of and the entrance to the spirit world, and it has roughly these three parts.

The Hell of Villains is situated in a relatively shallow part of the underworld. It is a place where the sunlight only comes in with a shadowy glow.

Repeating the fear of being killed

"Villains" would refer to people related to gangs or those who are quick to use violence. For adults it could be the *yakuza* or organized-crime syndicates, and for the young it would be delinquents who often use violence, like punching or kicking people, besides committing other wrongdoings.

What kind of world is the Hell of Villains that Princess Kozakura saw? In her spiritual message she talks of an unpleasant, foul-smelling river nearby. I suppose it is similar to a flow of sewage or wastewater. She then describes the dead bodies in the shallows, one of which has an upstretched hand, but she soon sees that they are not corpses but are actually alive and squirming underwater. And she tells us what happened after that: how a few dozen people shout at and chase after a couple from upriver, and catch and tie them to the foot of a bridge; the couple are then killed with sharpened broadswords. She describes such a fearful event.

The victims were actually a pair of lovers while alive, who were forbidden to marry and eloped, but ultimately committed suicide together. Maybe their fears were strongly felt when they ran away. These fears actually made them see the attackers who ran after them as red ogres. That is why they were chased, beaten, kicked and finally cut by swords in the underworld.

The Hell of Villains is characterized by the fact that one cannot die despite suffering the act of being killed, because the inhabitants do not have physical bodies, just like in other realms in the underworld. However, the parties concerned still believe they have physical bodies. A human soul is wrapped by its astral body, which takes the exact same shape as one's physical body. And because it has the same sensory abilities as the physical body, it can feel pain or the savagery of being killed when cut by a sword. So, the spirits believe they are dead, until they find themselves revived afterwards.

In this way, the Hell of Villains is a place where spirits repeatedly experience terror, from the period before death to the moment they die. Fear is one of the causal factors of hell.

Attracting that which you fear the most

Suicides of lovers may rarely occur today, but there are probably cases of those who abscond by night to flee from loan collectors. There may be some people who run under cover of night, slipping from place to place and end up dying hopelessly. Everybody around would seem like ogres from the standpoint of those who meet such an end.[*] In hell, what you fear will come after you; you will attract that which you fear the most.

Ogres do not really exist there. Those who like to torture or commit violence on others also fall to this realm, and they play the role of the so-called "sadists" or aggressors. In other words, hell is the stage for those who play the roles of sadists or aggressors, and oppositely those who play the roles of masochists or victims; both types exist, the ones who run away and ones who like to chase and give beatings.

In this world on Earth, there are people who run away in the night to escape loan repayments, while there are others who chase after them to collect the money. The latter includes the *yakuza*, or gangsters, and loan sharks who charge extremely high interest rates on personal loans and then go after people who cannot repay and flee. These gangsters and loan sharks will most likely take on the role of ogres in the other world after they die.

Criminals who ran from one hiding place to another while alive will also continue to run even after death. On the other hand, not all police officers who chased after people will go to heaven; some who are evil-hearted will fall to the underworld. They will continue chasing after others in the underworld as the ogres. So, roles are determined on fear.

---

* Even angels and bodhisattvas that have come to give a helping hand from the heaven may appear like ogres to them. The 10th-century Japanese Buddhist monk Genshin experienced the spiritual journey into the other world and reported that ogres were lecturing the souls in hell; but most of them were in fact angels and bodhisattvas.

The suffering of not being able to die

The spirits in the Hell of Villains experience the suffering of not being able to die. In most cases, they did not believe in eternal life while they were alive. This is why the attackers find that their victims do not die after their aggression, and the intended victims find that they do not die after a murderous act was done to them. They repeat these experiences.

Those who commit suicide by jumping from heights will have a similar experience. There are people who are deeply despaired for different reasons like loan problems, business failure, troubled personal relations, or their physical condition, and develop a loathing for their lives. They take their own lives wishing to disappear completely. However, these people will be surprised to see they are still alive despite having committed suicide, and then try it again in the other world, believing their first attempt had failed. And again, after a while, they come back to life. No matter how many times they try, they always come back to life. They repeat this over and over. There is such a kind of hell in the vicinity of the Hell of Villains. The spirits cannot die.

In the world on Earth, materialistic people who say there is no such thing as the other world nor believe in spirits make up the mainstream, and may even be considered as intellectuals. Not believing in the existence of such things is considered quite common for those who have received a scholastic education and work in society. If perhaps you mention in a social setting that the other world exists, as do spiritual beings, then the general reaction would be to regard you as out of your mind, with claims that you are old-fashioned or believe in superstitions. However, this value system will be completely reversed in the afterlife. People who did not believe in the other world nor in their eternal existence will repeatedly experience situations where it is taught that life is eternal, until they truly understand it. This is such a very important lesson.

Certainly, as they try to commit suicide each time, again and again, tens or even hundreds of times, they will eventually start to question why they cannot die. When they jump and hit the ground, they look dead with their bodies shattered and covered in blood, but after a while their body is restored. Or, they will cut and kill another with a sword, only to see the other person come back to life. This is the kind of world they live in. As they repeat their actions, the killers, the killed, and the suicides will gradually understand the reality of not being able to die, that life is eternal.

When guiding angels appear

At first, these spirits will wonder if they have gone insane, or have entered a world of fantasy. They might ask themselves if they are delusional or in a dream. Indeed, they are without doubt in a "nightmare." It is similar to the nightmares we have in our dreams, but it is without end. They experience the fear of not being able to wake up from the nightmare and continually live that reality.

Those who did not have this kind of knowledge during their lifetime will probably find it impossible to comprehend what is happening. It is harsh, but they will be stranded, acting out the same experience until they themselves become aware of the reality. In this sense, it is similar to the process of enlightenment. The same situation continues until the very moment they begin to understand on their own what is going on and awaken to the Truth that people have souls that do not die, and that they are actually in the hell that they may have heard of in stories.

When that moment arrives, with perfect timing guiding angels or bodhisattvas will come to admonish and teach them. The guiding angels appear in various forms, as an elderly person for example, and give them a reprimand and have them repent for things they had done while they were alive.

Many Happy Science believers who passionately carry out activities in this world will most likely take up this sort of task after they die. In this life, they may sometimes fail in their missionary work or might not succeed in guiding others, but this kind of work will carry over to the next world. The challenge in your workbook will continue in the other world; if you did not accomplish something in this world, you will learn how to do it in the next. People who have failed in guiding others in this world will have to do so in the other world. Your work will continue. That is why I tell you to convey the Truth earlier, while you still can in this world. Unless you work hard and succeed in your lifetime in this world, you will have to take the work back to try it again in the other world.

People who did not believe in the spiritual Truth will not be able to easily understand it even when they return to the other world. It would take them, in terms of material world time, one or two hundred years to understand. In this sense, those who cannot understand the Truth, whether or not they were talented, highly intelligent, or graduated from good schools while in this world, are all ignorant, living in spiritual darkness, and lacking in wisdom from the perspective of Buddha's Truth. Those without a thorough understanding of the fundamental Truth will look truly foolish.

For this reason, it is essential to inform people of the Truth. To achieve that end, I have published a variety of books, given lectures on different topics, and encouraged believers to give books of Truth to others and to do missionary work.

The world of fear, which is opposite to love

The Hell of Villains is such a world as shown above. The description of Princess Kozakura's spiritual message dates from the 17th or 18th century, but the situation nowadays is pretty much the same except with some modern variations.

According to Princess Kozakura, this hell is governed by fear regarding the physical body, and fear is the greatest enemy that makes people unhappy. It may well be true. Some say the opposite of love is jealousy, while others say in some aspect it is fear. Mutual love is based on trust and a sense of security, so we could say the opposite of love is fear. In fact, having fear means nobody is there to save you, so there is an absence of love. In addition, you feel that everybody who approaches you will harm you, you feel that everybody is persecuting you.

The important points to remember here are: people's lives are eternal and that we need to create a harmonious world in which people love each other instead of harming one another. These kinds of awareness are essential. Happy Science teachings are based on the actual observation of the world of hell. We have been providing the indispensable teachings to people in advance to help them avoid going there. So it is important to encourage many to read Happy Science books and listen to the lectures. It is also important to encourage them to take part in our activities, including giving books of Truth.

Our activities are not for earthly goals; they entail the salvation of souls. Saving people's souls is an extremely important task. The reality is that even if we witness somebody being fatally attacked by an ogre in the other world, we cannot save his or her soul easily. There is no way of saving that soul unless the person attains a certain level of awareness on his or her own. The person will start to listen to others only when he or she becomes disgusted with what has been going on or realizes something is wrong. Even if I were to talk to these spirits, they would not listen to what I have to say. They need to perceive reality on their own and open their hearts. It is such a kind of world.

Princess Kozakura points out in her spiritual message that fear springs from thinking that everybody is trying to harm you, and therefore, those with a strong sense of fear are egotists. She then goes on to say, "These people constantly focus on how others have hurt or harmed them. But humans are all children of God and have everlasting life. We can say we are children of God when we love one another and believe in each other. It is essential to have this way of thinking." This is what Happy Science has also been teaching, but there are still many people who have yet to understand this Truth.

Moving on to the next phase

The Hell of Villains is located in a relatively shallow area, which is why many of the spirits seem to go on to their next circumstances after two or three hundred years. Some will repent while they are there and move to heaven; in this case heaven would be the Astral Realm in the same fourth dimension. Others will accumulate more demon-like behavior and fall down to an even deeper part of hell. As they engage in atrocious killings over a long time, they will find themselves dropping even farther down.

Among the runaways, too, those who further develop negative state of minds will in time find themselves sinking to a deeper area. As if descending in an elevator or being dragged into a hole that suddenly cracks open in the ground, they will fall to another area. The spirits will go to the next place that is intended for each one of them, a world upward for some and downward for others. In any case, it is important that first one must altogether tire of the slaughter. This shows how one's effort is valued, to some degree, in saving oneself.

Subterranean Hell:
Lonely Company Employees

Subterranean Hell, according to Princess Kozakura

Secondly, Princess Kozakura speaks of the Subterranean Hell.

Princess Kozakura: I'm now going to describe what is called the Subterranean Hell. There has not been much documentation or records regarding this hell. As the name suggests, it is a place where the inhabitants are confined in pitch-black soil; there are many who are suffocating, gasping for air. A closer look will show that each one is in a small hole like a mole, and is kneeling down in a space no wider than one meter (3 feet) in diameter. They are just gasping, scraping the soil with their hands. The holes are too small for them to turn around or stretch their legs.

What surprises me is that many of these individuals are modern company employees; they wear white dress shirts and ties. They are crouched on their knees in small vaults for some agonizing reason. This realm was actually formed as a result of the suffocating, regimented society of today. Simply put, it is characterized by anthropophobia, or the excessive fear of people or society; many of the burrow dwellers feel the need to escape from superiors or subordinates they dislike. Squatting alone in complete darkness, they symbolically resemble the company employees of today.

The inhabitants here cannot see each other. Each in their own underground capsule reminds me of small one-room apartments in certain cities in the earthly world; it is as if such apartments have been buried in the ground. This is a new type of hell, formed in contemporary times, and how to rescue these inhabitants is still a topic of much debate among the angels of light.

The majority of those confined tenants do not want to talk to anybody, which is very troublesome. Some businessmen pretend to be obedient and act like yes-men at work, while is isolating themselves from their families at home, rarely speaking to their wives or children, as the result of overtime work, frequent business trips, or having been posted away from family. Becoming worn down from this drawn out lifestyle, these people eventually desire to just remain still in pitch-black darkness with nobody else around, like moles.

They probably will stay there until they realize that essentially they are free to think whatever they want and that they are children of God filled with light. There is no way of helping them unless they become aware of the foolishness of suffering all alone, because they are the ones who have an utmost desire to be left alone. I can only pray that their number will not increase.

Excerpt from Vol. 26, *A Collection of Spiritual Messages by Ryuho Okawa*

People in shells

This is new information. Other than the spiritual message from Princess Kozakura, no Happy Science teachings talk of this realm, so we could say this is a finding of recent study. A hell specific to salaried workers has been formed, which suggests that it has only been decades since its formation.

Princess Kozakura secondly introduces the Subterranean Hell, where many suffer in suffocation in the dark underground confined in small burrows like moles. They may be similar to recluses, loners, autistic people, or shut-ins. They have a distrust of other people or society, or who have feelings of being victimized, they shut themselves up in their own shells, thinking, "I cannot trust anybody other than myself." This kind of feeling is somewhat understandable. The world where such spirits reside is called the Subterranean Hell. There is also another realm called the Hell of Isolation, and the two may partially overlap.

According to what Princess Kozakura saw in her spiritual vision, many of the inhabitants are modern salaried workers in dress shirts and ties. She describes their nesting holes as being similar to urban one-room flats buried in the ground. This makes sense. People today are less and less able to build relationships with others, resulting in more people being isolated and closing their hearts. For this reason, it is understandable that a hell of Isolation is formed for those who cannot understand that people can trust and love each other. In the other world, the mental picture in their minds becomes their reality, so the formation of this kind of place is quite possible.

The reason this type of hell is formed is certainly due to a sort of anthropophobia. There are many people who have a fear of other people in a suffocating, regulated society; they desperately want to escape from the superiors and subordinates they dislike. There may also be people who have failed in family relationships. Some may have entered the Hell of Isolation after experiencing their domestic lives fall apart. This kind of realm has formed in hell.

Modern society certainly allows for a strong tendency towards individualism, unlike in olden times. There is no problem if individualism is applied in a good direction, but if it goes astray, it can lead you to this kind of isolated world. It would be as if you are living all alone on an isolated island, even while in the midst of a large group of people. So, we need to be aware of the importance of "how to think."

Happy Science emphasizes the teachings of love as the primary step; we teach about fundamental love, or neighborly love, and giving love. You may well be able to understand why we put these teachings of love in the first stage. It is because these are very important teachings in modern society. The world today seems to be a boundless, emotionally-barren field in which the masses of people are alive, so we must make efforts to spread the teachings of love. These efforts will make the desert-like land rich in nutrition, allowing us to plant seeds of "trees" and "crops." We continue our activities to this end.

Getting out of the Subterranean Hell

According to Princess Kozakura, Subterranean Hell is the place where those who do not want to communicate with others reside. This feeling is quite common; you can probably find people who feel like this in any occupation. I imagine there are many such people even in top-tier companies.

People with such feelings will fall to the Subterranean Hell upon returning to the next world after death, and cocoon themselves in meter-wide cellars like moles, and again, it is very difficult to save these souls. I think they will probably remain in their holes for some time, until they get bored. They most probably do not believe in the existence of the other world and regard the earthly world to be the only place there is, which is why they just stay there. But eventually they will certainly get bored.

Their situation is similar to that of former President of Iraq Saddam Hussein* when he was hiding underground; he was later uncovered and captured by American forces. A man who was once the president of a nation and lived in the Presidential Palace ended up having to hide in a small concrete hole. He probably thought, "Everybody is my enemy. I'll be killed if I'm found." Inhabitants of the Subterranean Hell most likely have a similar mindset.

There may well be people who feel this way. They shut themselves away in their own hole, suffering their fear in silence. They stay there for a long time, hoping they will not be found. They believe bad things will happen to them if they are discovered. However, nothing will be resolved unless they open their hearts and eventually go outside. It would be difficult for angels to open a hole in a concrete wall with a pickax and pull them out. This is hardly possible, although I imagine quite a lot of people are in this state.

---

* Saddam Hussein (1937 – 2006) was arrested by American forces in 2003 during the Iraq War, and was executed in 2006. On February 4, 2013, Okawa conducted spiritual research of his whereabouts in the other world, and discovered that he is in the Hell of Isolation. See *The Just Cause in the Iraq War; Did Saddam Hussein Possess Weapons of Mass Destruction?* (Tokyo: HS Press, 2013).

The necessity for new teachings

It is all the more important that people study the Truth and assimilate it. There is no way of helping them unless they had some opportunity to know the Truth during their lifetimes. It is extremely difficult to save people who have been brainwashed by materialistic idea that there is no such thing as the afterworld. Therefore, regardless of any criticisms that cross our way, we must spread the Truth. This is the only way to save people.

A new religion is necessary to deal with newly formed realms of hell like this one. Just like new medicine is needed for a new type of illness, a new vaccine for a new type of influenza or epidemic, we definitely need new teachings adequate for each type of newly formed hell; otherwise, we cannot overcome these problems. So, spreading the Truth is extremely important.

The Subterranean Hell is not described anywhere besides the spiritual message from Princess Kozakura. She states that the inhabitants are not aware that they are essentially free in their hearts and that they are children of God filled with light. And they cannot leave those places until they realize these truths. This is sad.

However, just consider it. Imagine yourself going to save them in the other world, and you will see how difficult it is. Even if you try to pull them out of their holes, from their perspective you will only appear as an enemy who is trying to attack them. Most probably you will not succeed. They are like moles that resist exit, believing they will die in the sunlight. They fight against any effort to pull them out, so there is nothing you can do. Those who fall to this realm were already lonely with closed hearts while they were alive on Earth, which is why this sort of hell exists. So, we need to save people from loneliness.

The Hell of Mortar:
The Destination for Egoists

The Hell of Mortar, according to Princess Kozakura

Thirdly, Princess Kozakura speaks of the Hell of Mortar, an expression that is quite old-fashioned.

Princess Kozakura: This Hell of Mortar is also filled with fear, but if I were to describe it in a perverse way, it is quite "thrilling." There I see a giant mortar, a shape like the volcanic crater of Mount Aso in Kyushu. It is so huge that its diameter is well over a hundred meters (330 feet).

A pool of hot water simmers at the bottom of the mortar, occasionally belching smoke smelling of sulfur from its center. It may even seem as lava boiling up.

Inside are thousands of lost souls crowded together like a colony ants, trying to climb up the sides to escape from this giant bowl. But as everybody thinks only of themselves first, they pull down those above them by grabbing their ankles. This is repeated endlessly, which is why not even one soul can escape the Hell of Mortar no matter how long they try. They slide down the rocky surface, one after another, along with the dislodged stones.

These pitiful beings are apparently a group of egoists who, when they were alive, had no compassion or affection for others, kicking them down for their own gain. When I look at these individuals who are scrambling like ants to climb the crater walls in frantic sweat, I am surprised to see many major company executive types or scholarly types among them. They are people who mercilessly booted others out of the way in their competitive race on earth for academic achievement or career advancement, and are here now paying the price for their actions.

The sides of the mortar are not sloped so sharply; if everybody would only cooperate with each other, they could easily escape, one by one. However, many of them do not seem to understand the importance of helping each other even after several decades or hundreds of years. To me, the way out is so simple and easy, but they cannot see it; they are so preoccupied in saving themselves to listen to what I have to say. They just reject my words answering, "Don't say such worthless nonsense when I'm so busy."

Just like spirits in other parts of hell, there is virtually nothing we can do until each individual raises his or her awareness. We could only look on this group of lost souls helplessly.

Excerpt from Vol. 26, *A Collection of Spiritual Messages by Ryuho Okawa*

A fearful scene in the mouth of a volcano

According to conventional Buddhist ideas of hell, the Hell of Mortar seems to overlap with the Hell of Scorching Heat, which will be described later (section 6 of this chapter). In many cases the two are described as one, but Princess Kozakura speaks of them as separate and here she focuses on the Hell of Mortar in particular.

She describes it as being full of fear and "thrills," looking like the crater of Mt. Aso, with a mortar-shaped pit about a hundred meters in diameter. The hot boiling water and the sulfurous smelling smoke arising from the bottom of the pit suggest it is like the opening of a volcano. So I guess it is very similar to the Hell of Scorching Heat. In the deepest part of the mortar are boiling water, lava, and sulfur; this would make people fearful of falling and desperate to escape. Thousands of lost souls are heaped like ants, inside the mortar.

This situation is opposite that of the Hell of Isolation I spoke of earlier. The scene of the Hell of Mortar is similar to modern company employees bustling to commuter trains. During rush hour, businessmen pack into trains, wishing to pass everybody and reach their company as quickly as possible. The situation is quite similar in the Hell of Mortal; it looks as if inhabitants are crowded like ants, wishing to be the only one to get out of there. It could also be likened to a big mass of people all rushing in a particular direction; for example, people rushing to a bargain sale. I feel this hell symbolizes a modern trait of people, hustling toward some kind of benefit or gain, or swarming to something just like insects to sweet nectar.

The realm that reflects Ryunosuke Akutagawa's The Spider's Thread

According to Princess Kozakura, thousands of lost souls are trying to climb the cliffs to get out ahead of everybody else, and so they pull down those above them by grabbing their ankles. This situation is similar to the world described in Ryunosuke Akutagawa's novel, *The Spider's Thread*.

While Buddhism teaches that Paradise is governed by the Amitabha Buddha, in his novel it is Shakyamuni

Buddha that appears. The Buddha tries to save a man named Kandata from hell because Kandata did one good thing during his lifetime, which was letting go of a spider that he was about to kill. So the Buddha lowers a spider's thread to help Kandata out. Kandata climbs up the thread toward Paradise, but he is followed by other lost souls of hell. On seeing the spider's thread so thin and fragile blown by the wind, Kandata exclaims, "Hey you, don't follow me, or it will break! This thread is mine!" At that moment, the spider's thread breaks and Kandata falls back to hell.

Ryunosuke Akutagawa wrote this story quite skillfully, and what is happening in the hell of Mortar is similar. This is indeed another form of hell. Even though we want to save the inhabitants there, we cannot, because their selfishness and egotism are too strong. They want to be saved, and we want to help them. But when we try to help them, their egotistic attitude will show precedence, making our attempts end in failure.

It sometimes happens, for example, that when a fire breaks out in a movie theater, people push each other as they rush for the exit, only to trip and die by getting crushed in a human pile. Inward-opening doors will not open if a throng of people rush the exit, and many will die from suffocation, being unable to get outside. We occasionally hear of this kind of incident and, in fact, the Hell of Mortar is just like this. People can escape if they just do it in an orderly fashion but everybody dies because of their greedy desire to be first to get out.

This example is symbolic; you can probably understand this feeling. Everybody more or less has a feeling of wanting to be the only one to be saved, or may have a desire to be happy at any cost, even if others should remain unhappy. But this kind of feeling is certainly hellish. Your desire to be happy itself is of course undeniable, but you also need to have a desire for others to be happy as well. The idea of "happiness for oneself, as well as for others" is important. Wishing to be a little happier than another is the allowable level of desire one can have.

Wanting to be happy even at the cost of others' happiness will certainly lead to hell. On the other hand, wishing for others' happiness by sacrificing your own is not good either if this feeling becomes too extreme. Overly sacrificing yourself will ultimately lead you to be unhappy. Also, even if you claim that you will be okay as long as other people are happy, you may never know if the people you are talking about are truly happy. So over sacrificing oneself is too extreme. The best way of thinking is to desire both you and others to become happy.

This is what Happy Science has been teaching. We teach the importance of attaining happiness that carries over from this world to the next, and that benefiting oneself benefits others. To put it another way, it is better to have the mindset that aims for the realization of happiness for both oneself and others.

How to escape the Hell of Mortar

Those in the Hell of Mortar grab others' legs and pull them down. This behavior is a manifestation of their desire to make others unhappy because they themselves have no hope of becoming happy. This kind of hell is probably very common in modern competitive societies. I'm sure some may feel ashamed of themselves on hearing this. If you are a passive person and do not mind remaining unhappy when others achieve success, you will most likely be left behind in a competitive society.

Some unhappy people get satisfaction or feel relieved, when they see others with the same kind of misery. You may probably understand this feeling. I am sure everybody has experienced this feeling at least once in their lifetime. However, you should not settle for this mindset. It might be human instinct to develop this mindset, but it should not be left as it is.

It is important to make an effort to congratulate those who have had success or who have completed a wonderful achievement. Only by doing so can you be free from this hell. The attitude of disapproval of others' success or happiness will keep you confined there forever, because hatred will deeply infiltrate your subconscious mind, preventing you from being successful.

If you deny another's happiness by saying, for example, "I cannot allow him to become manager so soon," and criticize that person, you will not be able to become a manager yourself, because the idea of denying any promotion will sink deeply into your subconscious mind, blocking your own promotion. In the same manner, if you see somebody making a lot of money and say, "He must have cheated to be successful. It is unbearable. I wish somebody would steal his money or that he gets robbed," then you will also not be able to achieve wealth yourself; the reason is that if you did make a lot of money, a thief or a robber would be attracted to you, making your "wish" come true.

When friendship turns into the Hell of Mortar

This is a caution to people in modern societies. Looking at the earthly world from the viewpoint of the Hell of Mortar, there are many situations in modern societies that share these hellish qualities. While it is understandable that such mindsets can develop, you must work hard to overcome them. The attitude of congratulating those who have had success will help you get out of the mortar.

Suppose a vow is made among a group of female friends to pursue their careers without ever getting married, but then one of them suddenly announces her surprise marriage to a man she unexpectedly became involved with. This can be unforgivable for the rest of the group; they would certainly want to press her to answer why she abruptly decided to marry when they all pledged to stay single their entire lives. The answer may be as simple as, "Well, one day he asked me out, and all of a sudden proposed to me, to which I answered 'yes.' That's about it." But it would still be unbearable. The others may certainly want to accuse her and remark, "There's nothing good about marriage. You'll only be unhappy."

In this case, too, accusing her will not lead to a solution of the situation. The other friends may cluster around the woman who is engaged, and criticize her or try to persuade her to refrain from marrying by listing all the reasons why she should stay single. They may surround her in a coffee shop, and say the hostile things like, "Your marriage will mean the end of your career," "Child-raising is hard work. It costs a lot these days," or "Your husband will soon cheat on you." Urging her to quit her marriage in this way will certainly create the Hell of Mortar.

To prevent this from happening, it is important to congratulate the one who is going to marry, even if she is one of the close friends who had mutually promised each other to remain single, and say, "I'm happy for you." Then, when such a circumstance may happen to you, you would be able to respond to the opportunity without hesitation.

The person who was paid respect will also be gladdened and, after marriage, will tell everybody around her that you are such a good-hearted person, who congratulated her sincerely when she least expected it instead of being negative as she may have anticipated. Her comments will create a good impression of you, and circulate to reach the appropriate people who might help you meet the right potential partner. This can happen. So, making an effort to celebrate other people's happiness is a way to prevent the Hell of Mortar from forming.

Those who fall to hell in a competitive society, And those who don't

The same is true with career promotions. When you compete for a promotion with a colleague who entered the company at the same time as you, you will feel quite upset seeing him or her get the promotion. You may have bad words for him or her, or complain that it is unfair, but in this case too, it is essential that you congratulate your colleague.

The person newly promoted is usually quite nervous, or anxious of how others might feel, including whether his or her peers are jealous. There might be worry that other people are complaining, saying, "The choice was made for the promotion even though others were also working hard. Maybe there was a special connection to one of the executives. The promotion came in return for a personal favor or due to some consideration out of work."

However, it is good to give the person positive comments like, "Congratulations. You worked really hard so that you deserve to be promoted to manager."

If, instead, you downplay the person's achievement with remarks like, "That guy just had good luck," "He knew how to swim with the tide," "He was good at buttering up his superiors," or "He got on the boss's good side by accompanying him to his favorite bar and entertaining him with the same karaoke songs he likes," then you will miss the chance to get promoted. The Hell of Mortar can easily grow in any form by such ill feelings.

When this type of situation occurs, it is important to focus on the good points of the person who was promoted, and admire him or her for having them. Doing so will help you improve your state of mind. And if you remain calm and continue working hard with an unshakable mind, you will definitely be given a chance for promotion within a year or two. The world can be a fair place, for there will be also people who look at you and think, "I'm sorry that person didn't get promoted much earlier."

But if, on the other hand, you become very irritated by another's promotion, you are only confirming to others that you do not deserve to be promoted. If you lose control of your life with bad behavior such as continually getting drunk or abusing your family, your bad reputation will eventually come to the attention of your superiors, leaving you no hope for promotion. So, it is better to make a conscious effort to praise those who had been promoted.

Somebody who advances in the organization faster than you has a higher potential to become a leading figure in the company, and he or she may well help you get ahead at some future time. In this sense, praising such a person may also benefit you in many ways. When giving praise however, do not do so out of selfish desire or for personal gain. Try to honor the person sincerely from your heart, and praise his or her good points.

People want to be friends with those who understand and approve of their good attributes. This is how people usually think. You wouldn't want to develop a friendship with somebody who always criticizes you whenever you meet. This is a general rule of thumb, so be thoughtful on this point.

Princess Kozakura describes this Hell of Mortar is filled with egotistical ones who, when alive displayed no compassion or affection but instead kicked others down. Many of them looked like the company executives or scholar-type intellectuals. She then says that people who were heartless enough to pull others down while competing in entrance exams or promotion, find themselves in this hell and are paying the price for those actions. This makes sense.

The positive side of a competitive society is that competition works to prevent corruption or deterioration. Service suppliers competing with each other will greatly benefit the consumers who buy their services, but those who are engaged in competition need to be cautious to not develop a hellish state of mind. We need to know about the negative side of competition as well. Neutralizing its negative effect is essential.

How to avoid becoming a "crab" inside a bucket

If everybody is willing to help each other, they will be able to go beyond the inclined walls. For example, if one of them manages to reach the top of the crater, that person can extend a hand to pull the others out, one by one. In this way, everybody can work together to get out in an orderly way.

There is a similar story that comes to mind. It is about crabs inside a bucket. When crabs are placed inside a bucket, they will apparently grab the one who tries to get out with their pincers and pull it down. Maybe hell is not solely associated with humans; it probably exists for crabs as well. If a crab can get to the top of the bucket and pull the other crabs up, they can all manage to get out, one after another. But all they do in reality is pull the one above them down. This is not a pleasant scene to watch. As stated by the proverb, "Learn wisdom from the follies of others," we must correct our behavior by observing these crabs.

Princess Kozakura wonders why the inhabitants

there do not understand such a simple truth, but selfish egotists just can't see it. They hardly understand that the act of pulling others down will create a sustained hell.

It is said that if jealous feelings were organized into a social system, it would result in communism. While equality is a good thing, the idea of approving jealousy of those who honestly try to rise above others, and bringing them down is not good. This is a negative aspect of human character that is intrinsic to all, but we must work to nullify it.

Examples of the jealous crab tendency can also be found in the mass media. They are symbolic of our society's vulgarity; attempts are often made to drag people down even at the slightest perception of their getting ahead. Similarly, this trait can also be found in the work of tax offices in Japan. As if to accuse those who have made a lot of money for having done something wrong, tax officials will come to collect even more taxes. After one has already paid a large sum of taxes, they will look for other areas where taxes can be levied. We need to be wary of this tendency. It is essential to develop more of a heavenly sense of values.

In her spiritual message Princess Kozakura said she could only look helplessly upon the lost souls. They could not understand a simple truth; even if you tell them to help one another, they would not listen. Since they were so fully focused on how to save themselves, they would not listen to what others had to say. They just reject any advice as worthless and silly. Such pitiful lost souls reside in this hell. On seeing them Princess Kozakura concluded that what matters was our views on life while we live in this earthly world as human beings.

The Hell of Beasts:
Human Spirits Taking Animal Forms

The Hell of Beasts, according to Princess Kozakura

Fourthly, Princess Kozakura speaks about the Hell of Beasts.

Princess Kozakura: Let us now move on to the fourth realm of hell. In this place, people take animal forms—like horses, cows, birds, snakes, or pigs—but with human faces. They take the form of an animal that most matches their state of mind. There are even those who become bats flying in the night sky, and hang upside down in caves.

Souls who have come to the Hell of Beasts are those

who had lost their sense of dignity as human beings while living on Earth. This is the fate of people who lived only by their animal instincts and desires, believing themselves to be just physical beings. Those with strong suspicious natures turn into snake-like creatures, those who cannot resist their physical desires turn into dog-like creatures, and those who always deceive others turn into fox-like creatures. Together they form the Hell of Beasts.

The most notable point is that the majority of these people have come to believe they are animals after having spent hundreds of years there. This is the truth of the phenomenon of "being possessed by an animal spirit." The spirits in hell, who believe themselves to be snakes or foxes, possess people on Earth and make them suffer. That is why, when conducting sessions of spiritual channeling, psychic mediums sometimes start to speak in a human language as they move like a snake or take the posture of a fox but in most cases, it is in fact the spirit of a human who had fallen to the Hell of Beasts.

Genuine animal spirits also do exist, but only the very ancient animal spirits can speak a human language, and the spiritual disturbances these spirits can make are often not so serious.

By possessing people on Earth, the spirits in the Hell of Beasts will veer off the human path even more, making it difficult to return to the bright heavenly world.

Excerpt from Vol. 26, *A Collection of Spiritual Messages by Ryuho Okawa*

The characteristics of those in the Hell of Beasts

"Hell of Beasts" is a unique expression; it is often called the Beast Realm or the Animal Realm. This hell also appears in another novel by Ryunosuke Akutagawa: *Toshishun*.

The protagonist Toshishun decides to apprentice with a hermit-sage. The hermit sage orders him not to speak a single word as part of his disciplinary training. During his training, Toshishun's soul depart his body and visits the other world. He then goes down to hell, where he meets his deceased parents who had turned into horses with human faces. Although Toshishun had been ordered not to speak, he cannot resist and calls out, "Mother!" At that moment, his soul is taken back to the earthly world. The hermit-sage then tells Toshishun that if he had said nothing in that instance, he would have been a failure as a human. This is the storyline of the novel.

So, why do humans turn into animals? It is because, in the other world, souls take the forms that correspond to their state of mind. One's outside appearance is the reflection of his or her mind; it is the manifestation of one's mental state.

This is true not only in the other world; in this earthly world, too, people's faces gradually change to reflect their characters. For example, some people develop a stern face, while others come to resemble animals. The faces of greedy people, or those of gluttons, sometimes look like that of animals. The movie, "Spirited Away" (released in 2001 by Toho and Studio Ghibli) depicts a scene in which the protagonist's parents turn into pigs, eating greedily. Sometimes a gluttonous person who is devouring food does indeed look like a pig, though this is not a kind observation. A pig is indeed a symbol for greed.

People with strong feelings of jealousy and suspicion sometimes manifest a character that is snake-like. Their faces and eyes also start to resemble those of a snake, as they outwardly display jealousy and suspicion. People with a strong tendency to steal things or take what belongs to others to make them their own, have a dog-like nature in animal terms.

Other than these, there are also many animals that have a strong sense of fear. Some animals readily run away because they are so fearful, while others like to hide in dark, damp places. Different animals have different characteristics, each representing a specific symbol. It is said that lions symbolize bravery, while sheep represent peace, and in this way, each animal represents some trait. That is why there is even a theory that states that God created different types of animals in order to show us the kinds of different natures our minds can take.

Considering the characteristics of each animal, we can certainly see different tendencies. And these tendencies can be found in humans as well, given that humans have the freedom of thoughts. If you look into your mind and find any tendency that resembles a specific animal, you need to reflect on that tendency and try to correct it. Otherwise, when you return to the other world after death and your mind is expressed freely, you can possibly take the shape of that animal.

In a love relationship, too, if you become mad with jealousy and bind so much as to torment the other, stalking him or her obsessively, it will seem as if you have become a big serpent. Your state of mind will closely resemble the nature of a serpent. So, once you find that your state of mind is similar to a type of animal, you should practice self-reflection. Otherwise, that tendency can lead you further astray.

How to avoid the Hell of Beasts

There is a definite line that separates humans from animals. There is such a thing as "minimum enlightenment as a human being," and we need at least to attain this level. To be free of an animalistic nature, it is very important to elevate our spirituality by practicing self-reflection, meditation, and prayer. If we live materialistic lives in this modern society without practicing these activities and instead let ourselves be led by our desires, we will soon find ourselves directly connected to this Hell of Beasts.

In packed commuter trains, for example, there are sometimes cases of molestation. Probably 99 percent of men may be tempted to touch women's breasts or buttocks if they happen to be right in front of them. But if they do not even feel the slightest hesitation arising from their conflicted soul to stop the act, they are wrong. The molester might think he has a chance to touch a woman for free. He would have to pay quite a bit if he went to a place that employed "professional" women, so he might look forward to his daily commute so he could touch women for free. There may well be such men. Indeed, their problem is they lack humanity in the sense that they do not understand the feelings of others.

How does the victim feel? She would probably develop a strong loathing of commuting by train. If she happens to encounter such men every day, her sense of loathing will certainly last the entire day and would prevent her from concentrating on anything else. It is essential to put yourself in the other person's shoes.

Nevertheless, the same action can lead to heaven as well as hell, depending on what is intended. In a loving relationship, for example, a woman may feel sad if her partner does not even touch her hand after being together for a year. She may complain, "My boyfriend is cold-hearted. Even after we have dated for a year, he still hasn't held my hand, let alone kiss me. He absolutely shows no physical affection to me. I wouldn't shout out that he was doing something wrong, so why doesn't he hold my hand?" Between people with affection for one another, such physical behavior can be heavenly, an act to prove your love to your partner. In this way, even if the act itself is similar, the spiritual value will differ depending on what is in one's mind.

Those who commit repeated acts of molestation have a nature that is attuned to the Hell of Beasts. They will probably become more animal-like. This is something we should know about. It is sad, but there are people who, despite having been born human, take the form of an animal after death.

The Hell of Beasts is often found in the Indian teachings of reincarnation. When referring to reincarnation in India, it doesn't mean being reborn in this world; it rather means being reborn in the other world 49 days after one's passing from this one. It is the same in Tibet. Buddhism also teaches the idea that people's souls return to the other world after death but will wander about for 49 days, not knowing their destination. After this period they will be reborn in one of the realms in heaven or hell. This notion of "49 days after death" exists in Japan as well. In fact, they teach that people not only are reborn in physical form, but also as spirits. Although the meaning of the expression, "being reborn" is indistinguishable between the two, people in India or Tibet often speak of being born in the spirit world.

What about Western philosophy or religion? Although the idea of reincarnation is thought to be refuted, it does exist in the West, too. Plato writes in *The Republic* that people's souls receive sentencing by judges and are guided to openings leading to heaven or hell, and after serving a period of time in either of the two places, could return to this world and choose the form of life they wanted to live; one soul chose to live the life of a swan. Thus, people's souls are reborn in the other world after death, where one takes the form that reflects what is in one's mind. This is worthy to note.

In order to escape the Hell of Beasts, it is indispensable to attain an enlightenment in which we are aware that in the other world, we take the form that corresponds to our own minds and we go to the realm that accords with our state of mind.* This truth is now only taught at Happy Science. Long-standing religions including traditional Buddhism and Christianity, do not teach this in a clear manner, but you can study this through Happy Science teachings.

It is indeed true that your outward appearance will change according to your thoughts. For example, a married

---

* Souls in the Hell of Beasts will be able to return to a human form if they awaken to the basic truth. But as they spend two to three hundred years in the Hell of Beasts, some will forget that they were once humans. Sometimes these souls will incarnate as animals in their next lives in order to learn how grateful it is to be humans. Although in rare cases, they will incarnate as reptiles, such as snakes, in most cases they will be born as mammals, such as pet dogs, and observe humans as they live nearby.

woman will look like a demon if she is crazy with anger. In spiritual terms, it will appear like her mouth widens to her ears and horns grow out of her head. She may well look like a demon or ogre when she believes something is suspicious and accuses her husband angrily, saying, "What have you been up to, coming home so late at night? What's this lip mark on your collar? Who's lighter is this? And whose are those cigarettes? You didn't have them when you left home this morning." Conversely, when given a present, such as a ring, she treats her husband kindly like an angel. The same person can change in this way.

If your anger manifests in the other world and it becomes your nature, your appearance will change in accordance with that nature. This is something horrifying. But outcomes can go to this extreme, because we are given freedom and have to take responsibility for how we use that freedom. Living in modern society, we need to reflect on this point to avoid such a consequence.

The meaning of our being born into this world

In her spiritual message, Princess Kozakura gives her opinion that eternal life is truly a blessing for those who live in an admirable manner, yet it is utter eternal torture for those who suffer in anguish in hell. She also says that humans must be "selfish" in the truest sense; truly selfish people will strive to live their eternal life in happiness.

In order to live eternal lives of happiness in both this world and the other, we need to refrain from sowing the seeds of unhappiness. Everybody has been given the freedom of thoughts, so we can think whatever and however we want. But we are expected to choose the good thoughts. In the process of distinguishing heavenly thoughts from hellish ones and actually choosing the heavenly ones, our judgment between what is good and evil becomes more discerning, thereby producing wisdom. This wisdom, which is the result of the process of choosing heavenly thoughts, is a valuable treasure.

Some people may argue that it would be better for us to be able to choose only among good options, but that in a sense would be denying freedom. It would severely restrict our freedom. What is more, the meaning of our being born into this world would mostly be lost.

Humans repeat the cycle of being born into this world from the other, and then returning to the other world from this one. That is because of the dominant idea that life in this world on Earth is a setting that works to advance the evolution of the soul. This world is beautifully made as a stage for the enhancement and refinement of souls. In this world, different values co-exist, from which humans can freely choose. As a result, success and failure are produced. Through this experience, souls are trained and polished, producing yet further successes or failures. Without this world on Earth, the other world will stagnate. In that case, the eternal world would mean eternal stagnation. That is why souls occasionally come down to Earth to experience earthly lives.

The danger of Inari worship

One of the reasons the Hell of Beasts, or the Animal Realm, has come into being is probably the practice of animal worship. In Japan, there are many shrines that worship the spirits of animals, such as Inari, the fox deity[*], or others like snakes. Inari worship, for example, can be found throughout Tokyo, one of which is Inari Daimyojin Shrine in Shinjuku, central Tokyo. If you pray at places like this for worldly benefits, such as success in business, "something" will hear your prayer and approach you.

This "something" is not necessarily the Inari Daimyojin or a fox spirit, partly because foxes are not so

---

[*] While Inari is now considered the worship of the fox deity, it was originally the worship of a god of agriculture and foodstuff, such as to the god *Uka-no-mitama-no-kami*, to which people would pray for an abundant harvest, and foxes were thought to be the messengers of the god Inari. As time passed, however, people started to pray for worldly benefits, including success in business and family safety, and they even started to believe the god Inari to be a fox. At present, there are about 30,000 Inari shrines in Japan.

prevalent nowadays. In many cases, it is most probably a spirit that once had been a human living on Earth but who had fallen to the Hell of Beasts after death due to animalistic desires, like those of a fox. And if you selfishly pray to achieve some materialistic desire or to increase your company's sales, for example, such beings will come to possess you.

As in the Japanese saying, "Far from god, far from his curse (Let sleeping dogs lie)," sometimes it is better to not approach a place serving as a shrine for an animal, because it can be dangerous. People have faith in animal deities, and their faith works to amplify the power of the spirits there. Even if the spirits imitate fox mannerisms and may appear like foxes, in most cases they are human spirits. It is hard to imagine that fox spirits actually have the power to grant divine favors to people on Earth in response to their Inari worship. In the majority of cases, that which appears is a human spirit who has fallen to the Hell of Beasts and has taken the form of a fox.

So what are the characteristics of foxes? Firstly, they are very scheming; they have the ability to deceive people by lying or speaking deceptively. Secondly, they have strong desires. Thirdly, they are suspicious. That is why they are drawn to people who desire to earn money by even deceiving others. Those with such a tendency need to be wary of this. There is something frightening about Inari worship.

Encountering a snake spirit

What about snake deity worship? I personally find it unpleasant and do not favor the worship of snakes, but there are people who do worship them, which is frightening.

I have mentioned earlier that one spring I had travelled from Mt. Koya in Wakayama Prefecture to Yoshino in Nara Prefecture, which is famous for its beautiful cherry blossoms. On my visit to the site, I had the following experience.

There was a mountain valley there, and at the bottom of the valley I found a shrine for the worship of the "Grand Noten Deity." "Noten" literally means top of the head. I wondered what it meant, and soon found out that it was a shrine for a snake whose head had split apart. It was unpleasant to look at. Apparently, a story had been told since long ago that there was a snake whose head split apart and died; but then it appeared in the dream of a person who was told to build a shrine for it. That is how it came to be worshiped.

After learning this, I regretted visiting the site. I wanted to avoid having the snake spirit appear before me. But when I returned to my hotel later, the snake spirit did appear before me. This kind of shrine usually has some kind of spirit lingering around it. Although I wanted nothing to do with the worship of a split-headed snake, its spirit did appear so I rebuked it severely, telling it to stop doing wrong.

This snake spirit had become bloated with pride because of its worship by humans. Since it had become the object of people's faith, it had gained some spiritual power. Be it snake, fox, or other animal, if it becomes the center of people's faith, it gains the spiritual power to vent its resentment and commits many kinds of bad acts, including putting curses on living people. I strongly condemned the snake spirit because it had definitely been doing evil things by possessing people.

Visiting strange shrines can often bring about later misfortune, like illness or troubles arising in the family, caused by the spiritual possession of evil spirits. So it is best to stay away from them. Even among shrines and temples, there can be suspicious places where the thought energy of people's desires whirl about, or which have become nesting places for many evil spirits. If you visit such places and offer prayers to achieve your desires, you may easily become possessed so you need to be careful. Imagine the mindset of animals, and you will get the basic idea of what kind of thoughts would connect to what kind of animal spirits.

Animal spirits are best to be avoided. When I was working at a trading company, there was a colleague who was possessed by a "dog deity" or something similar to a dog spirit. When golfing, everybody he played with would comment that he cheated on his golf score, taking off a stroke here and there. You might well imagine this kind of mindset does not matter so much, but it certainly would be attuned to the mind of a dog. The existence of animals with different natures is probably meant for providing us some lessons, but once born as humans, we want to remain humans.

6

The Hell of Scorching Heat: A Destination for Greedy People

The Hell of Scorching Heat, According to Princess Kozakura

Fifthly, Princess Kozakura speaks about the Hell of Scorching Heat.

Princess Kozakura: Tonight I'm going to guide you through the fifth place, the Hell of Scorching Heat. As the name suggests, here the inhabitants' bodies, or what they believe to be their physical bodies, are severely burned by intense heat. Men and women who are just skin and bones with only a cloth wrapped around each of their waists, wander around, seeking water in the shimmering heat of a desert.

This hell is characterized by the word "craving." It is the destination of people who have forgotten about giving to others and have lived their lives with greed, only seeking things from others. They had strong desires for material things, living their lives never satisfied and never content. These people's thoughts create the psychological landscape of a scorching desert where hot winds blow constantly.

Those in this Hell of Scorching Heat can be saved only if they practice two things. One is to practice offering, which means carrying out acts of love for other people. The other is to live every day without being swayed by desires, but to have contentment in their hearts. People who know how to be content, and take steady steps each day with the awareness of their own missions, have no connection with hell. But foolish are those who are at the mercy of their multitude of desires and try to obtain whatever they want, thereby torment themselves on their own.

Therefore, the Hell of Scorching Heat is definitely not a place God created to punish humans. This particular environment actually serves to be a shortcut to enlightenment for its inhabitants. Lost spirits can attain a higher level of enlightenment by pondering the reason why they are in the Hell of Scorching Heat.

Excerpt from Vol. 26, *A Collection of Spiritual Messages by Ryuho Okawa*

A hot world of "craving" like a burning desert

As mentioned earlier, the Hell of Scorching Heat of which Princess Kozakura speaks is more like a realm that is a burning desert; in the heat haze of a desert, those who have been reduced to skeletons are craving water. The characteristic of the Hell of Scorching Heat is the heart that only craves. People with no thought of giving but only greedily covet and take from others, will go to this desert-like place. The sun blazes in the desert, making them thirsty. This is the destination of the people who are thirsty with selfish desires.

There is of course no problem with temporary heat, as some people willingly pay to go into a sauna; it feels refreshing to enjoy a sauna for ten or twenty minutes. However, if you were forced to stay in a sauna forever, then it would be a terrible "scorching heat." Imagine how it feels like to live in a sauna for a long time; it would be unbearable. Although ten to twenty minutes of sweating might be okay, you can never feel any cool breezes nor find any oasis in the Hell of Scorching Heat.

Those who constantly crave things and only take love will go there. There are things people cannot understand unless they learn religious teachings. Modern society is a society of desires, in which people cannot stop their craving for things they want. But religions teach the pain of not being able to obtain what one wants. Unless you know this truth, you cannot put an end to your desires.

The heat-related hell can take different forms. This desert-like place is one example. There is also the one that has formed like the mortar-shaped volcanic Mount Aso, described in Section Four of this chapter. There are different variations, which together are called the Eight Great Hells[*]. As opposed to a hot hell, there is a cold one as well, which also has different types. Religions originating in hot regions like desert areas regard heat as something hellish, which is why they often refer to a heat-related hell. On the contrary, religions in cold regions do not often speak of a hot hell. This makes sense.

The psychological landscape formed in the Hell of Scorching Heat is a torrid desert where hot winds are blowing. The Real World, or the other world, is a place where you cannot lie to your own heart, and what is in your mind is accurately manifested both by your physical appearance and in your environment. There, your heart is transparent like glass, and you cannot tell a lie or be untruthful.

According to Princess Kozakura, practicing self-reflection by discovering the clouds over your mind and

---

[*] The Eight Great Hells, otherwise known as Eight Hot Hells, include *Samjiva* (reviving), *Kalasutra* (black ropes), *Samghata* (crushing), *Raurava* (screaming), *Maharaurava* (great screaming), *Tapana* (heating), *Pratapana* (scorching heating), and *Avici* (abyss), though there are different theories.

removing them is essential. She says, "No one can be free of committing any sins. It is impossible to live an entire life without ever committing a single sin. This is why we are taught to practice self-reflection."

While it is possible to deceive oneself or others in this earthly world, we cannot do so in the other world, because what is in our mind will show directly in our environment as well as in our appearance. This is frightening. The obsessive mind that is filled with selfish desires will be attuned to the Hell of Scorching Heat, and those who had lived their lives in this state of mind will be burned there after death. There is also a similar one, called the Hell of Flames, where there are intense fires. This is also a place where people with excessive desires go.[*] It is another painful world, where people are burned in the flames of desire.

---

[*] In addition to those with excessive desires, people with strong anger, hatred, and aggression will also go to the Hell of Flames after death. Spiritual investigation of Happy Science has revealed that the following people currently find themselves there: The 2nd president of the Japanese religious group Soka Gakkai, Josei Toda (1900 - 1958) and the founder of the Japanese religious group Sukyo Mahikari, Koutama Okada (1901 - 1974). Josei Toda was a very aggressive person. He denied all religions other than his own, and encouraged his believers nationwide to force people to convert to his religious group. Koutama Okada mislead people by teaching wrong idea that with a special pendant known as *Omitama*, one can receive God's light and save others by raising their hand over them and radiating the light from the palm of their hand. This idea is wrong because we can only receive God's light by undergoing spiritual training and purifying our minds. While spiritual phenomenon may occur in his religious group, the majority of them are caused by evil spirits, which entails the danger of being possessed by them.

How to escape the Hell of Scorching Heat

To escape there, it is important to put out the flames of desires. Every living creature certainly needs to have a certain amount of desires to survive, but if your desires become excessive enough to make others suffer or deteriorate the world, then, after death you will find yourself in a place in which you will be burned in the flames of your desires. To avoid this, it is essential to know how to be content and have love and gratitude toward other people. You also need to be humble.

Happy Science teaches the importance of "Happiness Planting," or making offerings in many ways, such as donating money and generously giving to charity. Nurturing the heart of offering is an important practice in our spiritual training so as not to go to a place like the Hell of Scorching Heat. If you are preoccupied with taking or stealing from others without ever giving, you will end up in such a place after death.

It is a heavenly practice to spare some of your money and put it toward spreading the Truth, holy missionary work, and saving many people, while restraining your desire for more money. Thus, the practices of monetary contribution, generous charity work, and "Happiness Planting," are all valuable practices of spiritual training to avoid going to the world of desires. To extinguish the flames of desire, you need to provide something positive, as opposed to negative. That means you need to have a heart of giving, to give something to help others while restraining your own desires. This, in fact, is the way to escape the Hell of Scorching Heat.

It accords with the law of cause and effect that after death, the flames of worldly delusion and desires will burn people who thought only of themselves during their lives; this is a natural consequence. So it is important to know how to be content and be grateful for what we have been given. Continually teaching people this truth is also part of our important work.

People in modern society, in particular, need to know this, because while they are good at making assertions of what they lack, they are not really aware of what has been given to them. Take, for example, having an occupation. When people are laid off and lose their jobs, they understand for the first time how important their jobs had been to them. But when they were working, they only complained about how others earned a higher salary, or how others had been promoted ahead of them. Only when they lose their jobs can they understand how grateful they should have been to have had a job in the first place. They should feel more grateful for being able to have a job.

The Realm of Devils:
Inhabited by Evil Leaders

The Realm of Devils,
According to Princess Kozakura

Sixthly, Princess Kozakura speaks of the Realm of Devils.

Princess Kozakura: I will now introduce another place that is even more hellish. This is generally called the Realm of Devils, where spirits more atrocious than normal evil spirits reside. Their activities can roughly be broken down into two categories. One is to attract many minions in the underworld in order to take the positions of power in every part of hell. The second is to escape to the world on Earth and do evil deeds using other evil spirits.

Let us consider their first activity. I have so far spoken about the Hell of Villains, the Subterranean Hell, the Hell of Mortar, the Hell of Beasts, and the Hell of Scorching Heat. Other than the above, there are also notable ones such as the Hell of Lust[*] and the Abysmal Hell[†]. In each hell, there is a Satan-like boss, and those from the Realm of Devils fulfill these roles. They believe they are ruling over the dark world, in their own way, waiting for a chance to deal a blow to the angels of light.

Their most distinctive feature is their strong belief in power; or more accurately, an inexhaustible desire for power, a desire for whatever they want, be it some material thing or a person. Once humans taste power and become drunk with it, it is hard to forget its taste. Their divine nature as humans will become seared. While humility and modesty are essential for human beings who are children of God, these two qualities are completely lost on those in the Realm of Devils.

Let me say some words concerning their second activity as well. They are purposely trying to lead the world on Earth in the direction of chaos and destruction. Crazed groups that continually cause repeated strife on Earth are, without exception, manipulated by these beings. They are always active in the background of extreme right or left wing individuals that are fiercely belligerent, or of people belonging to misguided labor union movements.

---

* The Hell of Lust is a destination for those who committed mistaken sexual acts and were led by lust, like having extramarital affairs. They anguish in a pond of blood, which is why this hell is also known as the Hell of Bloody Pond.

† Abysmal Hell (or *Avici* in Sanscrit) is the lowest part of hell, the destination of leaders including philosophers, religious leaders, politicians, and business owners, who have deluded many people through mistaken philosophy. It is isolated like a jail, detached from the rest of the world, so one that is put there will not negatively influence other spirits.

These beings know the most efficient ways to spread chaos on this earthly world. That is to say, they foster insane religious leaders to delude society. This is the underlying reason why it is said that evil will rise when angels of light descend to this earthly world to preach the Laws. The beings of the Realm of Devils will actively try to make people confused between what is true and what is false, thereby plunging the earthly world into confusion in the spiritual sense. Fighting them and possibly even guiding these beings to the heavenly world is the work of the guiding spirits of light who have descended to Earth.

Excerpt from Vol. 26, *A Collection of Spiritual Messages by Ryuho Okawa*

Even devils play a necessary role

"Realm of Devils" is another term that first appeared in the Spiritual Message from Princess Kozakura; it doesn't appear in other books. The Realm of Devils means a place where devils reside, but since devils exist in each realm of hell, it doesn't necessarily mean that all the devils are gathered in one place.

Devils appear as bosses in the different parts of hell. They each have their own "command post" where they play "necessary" roles; in fact, by ordering evil spirits to do even more atrocious acts, they provide the latter a chance to reflect on their past behavior. It can be likened to the world of organized crime; members may sometimes want to quit the group because of its involvement in acts that are so cruel and merciless. Those in the underground society will not respond to any suggestion to do good, but as they continue to commit increasingly evil acts, some will eventually come to find it unbearable as humans and want to disobey. In this way, they begin reflecting on their past and repent.

Devils are beings who aggressively engage in evil

Devils provoke extremely evil acts. If possessed by them, the victim will often hear the words, "I will kill you." Though human beings are endowed with an eternal life, when devils make their appearance on Earth, their words are usually, "I will kill you." This is their distinctive feature.

There are many patients in mental hospitals who hear the voice of spirits. They apparently often hear voices, saying such things as, "I'll kill you," "I'll curse you," or "I'll make you miserable." These people have actually developed spiritual inclinations, but are only susceptible to evil spirits and are completely attuned to them.

Devils utter these kinds of curses and scheme to bring unhappiness to others. You may be surprised to hear such a mindset exists, but this feeling is also in the hearts of living people. In this world on Earth, there are people who purposely commit wrongdoings. They can be acts of independent individuals, as well as acts by groups of people. Sometimes people get together and conspire to do wrong as a team.

For example, there are cases in which delinquent youths get together and beat a homeless person to death, or gather in secret places to take drugs, knowing it is a wrongful thing to do. In places where evil is rampant, there will always be leaders who encourage wrongdoings; they believe in the power of evil and take much pleasure in getting others to follow their orders.

In Japan, there was a cult called Aum Shinrikyo, which later changed its name to "Aleph." There still are followers who cannot break away from this group, believing it is a reasonable religion. It certainly is a religion, but one that has been led by a devil. A devil-led group of believers is, in a way, also very "religious"; many spiritual phenomena can occur and people's wishes will also be accomplished in the form of curses. We have seen the example of a "living devil" in the Aum incident.[*] The founder of Aum Shinrikyo, Shoko Asahara, will be a real devil after his death.[†]

---

[*] The Aum incident refers to the series of crimes committed by the group. The most notorious was the Tokyo subway sarin attack on March 20, 1995; members of Aum Shinrikyo released sarin gas on three Tokyo subway lines, which caused the deaths of 13 people and injured 6,300.

[†] Shoko Asahara was convicted for being the mastermind of the Tokyo subway sarin attack and was sentenced to death in 2016. On July 6, 2018, the day of his execution, Happy Science recorded a spiritual message from his spirit. From its content, we are almost certain that his destination after death would be the Abysmal Hell.

That type of person will not change his mind even in hell. Nevertheless, this is one of the innate tendencies of humans; we need to recognize this as one possible pattern of behavior.

Devils' way of thinking

Those who had a strong influence in this world making people unhappy tend to become devils after death. Additionally, if they were central objects of faith in a religious group, they will gain extremely strong spiritual power, and their wrongdoings will not end.

This is horrible; they are to be pitied as humans. They live in a world that is based on absolute hatred and resentment, the exact opposite of the teachings of love. But this negativity is the byproduct of the freedom of the human mind. It is sad, but you probably have this same tendency. Everybody has this impulse in his or her own mind, so we should be careful not to amplify it. It is natural that people have a desire for power, and a desire to control others and objects in any manner they please. If this desire becomes too intense and exceeds the level you deserve, you will unfortunately enter the domain of devils.

For example, Hitler restored Germany from the devastation of World War I in a short period of time.

8

Using Freedom Correctly

This chapter was mainly focused on discussions of the underworld communicated through the spirit of Princess Kozakura. This is an extremely important topic. Though I do not want to frighten people, I think it is worth talking about since hell actually does exist. This is by no means a lie or fabrication. Although the "Spiritual Message from Princess Kozakura—Part 1" did not mention, there are also other realms such as the Hell of Lust and the Abysmal Hell.

Hell is inevitably formed when people in this world go too far astray, beyond the bounds of what is allowed as humans. It is a matter of how you have used your freedom. It is the reverse side of having freedom, so it is inevitable. Take, for example, a kitchen knife. A knife is useful when you cook, but it shouldn't be used to kill somebody. While we have the freedom in determining how to use it, we must use it correctly with the power of wisdom. This world on Earth is the place to learn such wisdom.

This has been an introductory lecture on the world of hell. I would be happy if you deepen your understanding to better your future life.

◆ The true thoughts of devils who are Filled with the desire to dominate ◆

According to Happy Science spiritual research, Mao Zedong, the founder of communist China, Joseph Stalin, the former dictator of communist USSR, and Friedrich Nietzsche, the 19th century German philosopher who stated, "God is dead," became devils after death. Mao Zedong, in particular, is one of the most evil devils of the Earth.

Devils attempt to influence people on Earth into corruption and ruin. In order to make clear their schemes and prevent them from coming to fruition, Happy Science has published spiritual messages of these spirits regarded as devils. Below are excerpts from the spiritual messages of these three individuals.

◆ Mao Zedong (recorded on November 15, 2018)

- [Concerning Xinjiang, Tibet, and Inner Mongolia being invaded by and absorbed into China] That is the result of being weak. Being weak is a sin.
- [Concerning the massacre of Tibetans by China] It's nothing; it was just a million people, right?

- Well, Xinjiang is where a massacre is taking place now. With the deaths of a million people, the issue would pretty much be settled there.
- Religion should be used in any way we want in the best interest of the nation. Religions are merely "tools" of human invention.
- The bottom overthrows the top. That's why communism is the true "democracy."
- [Concerning human life and human rights] That's nonsense. Human life is insignificant in order to realize a just cause.
- It wouldn't take much effort to crush Taiwan. If we were really serious, it would be over in a month.
- If you want to make your country strong, you must eliminate the lower twenty percent or so. These people are just failures anyway.
- I will rule the world and bring equality to the workers of all lands.
- China has over a billion people and even as the majority of them are using smartphones or cell phones, we are able to control their information access. This is a perfect model for future society.
- [Concerning the people of China] We must never give them freedom. We can only restrict them. We have managed to turn 1.4 billion people into "slaves," so we must continue to keep up these efforts.

◆ Stalin (recorded on June 16, 2015)

- If you write something bad about me, you'll be shot dead.
- [Concerning Marxist thought] With Marxist thought we can support violent revolution. A revolution without violence is actually impossible. We can never achieve success without the use of weapons. So, just bring weapons when you go to protest. You should be armed.
- [Considering Chinese President Xi Jinping] Well, he has a good bearing. Yes, he has really sharp eyes. But I don't really support him. Because if I did, China would be stronger and Russia weaker. Ultimately, Russia must rule the world.
- The best scenario now is to have China and the U.S. fight each other to make them both weaker. When it becomes weak enough, we will occupy China. That is the best scenario.
- Anybody who is jealous of me is a bad person. Anybody who calls me "evil" is a bad person. Anybody who does not follow my orders is a bad person! [*slams desk*].

◆ Nietzsche (recorded on February 3, 2012)

- When I say "resentment," I am referring to the emotional reaction to all the unfulfilled desires people have accumulated over the years being rejected by society.

- How high can a person go? Feelings of resentment give one the energetic boost to attain something. People who are satisfied with their current situations lack that boost.
- (Interviewer: How much resentment do you have?) The most in the world.
- If humans did not have "the will to power,"* life would be meaningless. Power is the ultimate ability to make people obey you. If you can make a lot of people follow you, it means you have strong power. And that basically means you are close to God. God is actually power.
- [Concerning Beelzebub] He is very busy flying around the world. He has wings – beautiful jet black wings – to take him anywhere to carry out various activities. I am more suited to develop philosophy from my cave.
- [Concerning Lucifer] He is also busy so it is not easy to see him so often. Sometimes though, he might come to me to inquire about my teachings. But he is basically somebody of action. And conferring wisdom is my role. I am "God," so my role is conferring wisdom. And he takes that wisdom and puts it into action.

---

* "The will to power" is a central concept in Nietzsche's philosophy. According to his belief, everybody has the will for power; everybody wants to seek power to grow, spread, and expand their strength, and become dominant.

Chapter Two

An Exploration *into* The World of Hell

A Tour of Modern Hell Experienced During Sleep

1

A Journey into the Spirit World

Let me start by explaining what had happened to me that led me to give this talk, upon which this chapter is based. Quite honestly, I had no idea that I would be speaking on this topic until the very morning I gave the lecture. My original plan for that day was to make necessary decisions concerning the monthly reports of the Happy Science administration, and then hold interviews and meetings with management. So I was hoping to have a relaxed sleep the night before that day.

But "bad things" often happen at such times. As I was having trouble getting into a peaceful sleep, "it" started to happen. I thought, "Ah, here it comes." Then, from around 11:30 that night, my travel began. It was a journey into the spirit world, which started with the feeling of being spiritually dragged and I thought something was about to begin. It often happens when I least expect it. What's more, it usually happens at the most inopportune time.

The initial journey into the spirit world started around 11:30 pm and lasted for about two and a half hours until around 2:00 am. It would have been fine if my destination had been a good place, but I was taken to the underworld on this occasion, and that is how my tour around the world of hell started.

2

The *Ashura* Hell: Repeated Terrorism

I arrived at the scene of a train blowing up

The first place I was taken to was very different from the classic image of hell. So I was at first a little confused about where I was. Then I suddenly found myself in a place like the inside of a train. From within the train-like place, I could see a European-like landscape outside. In addition, passengers on the train looked European. I was looking around, wondering what was going to happen. Then I heard an explosion. A bomb exploded inside the train, and a scene looking exactly like the Hell of Agonizing Cries unfolded before my eyes. So I had arrived at a place where a tragedy was happening.

I guessed it was a kind of *Ashura* Realm[*], a world of strife and destruction, which was combined with the Hell of Scorching Heat. It was indeed extremely hot; a painfully burning heat pierced my right arm, which continued throughout my stay. It was a place of fiery heat and agonizing cries.

---

[*] In principle, *Ashura* Realm is formed as a result of war. However, one does not have to be associated with war to go there. Those who have a strong belligerent character or are controlled by their anger also go there.

Other than Europeans, I also saw people who looked Turkish and others who appeared Muslim. I thus had witnessed a blast and the horrifying sight of the blood bath that followed.

Where does the scorching heat come from?

Continuing the tour, I was then taken to various places that looked similar to where terrorism had occurred around the world. I walked through sites, one after another, where tragedy had happened; they were places of repeated terrorist attacks. It would be right to say that it was an ongoing hell, which parallels what has been unfolding on Earth. Terrorism occurs in various parts of the world, where buses and trains are blown up, and then there are the suicide bombings in the Middle East. Similar tragedies have taken place in the spirit world as well, though in slightly different forms, among those who harbor feelings of opposition, animosity, hatred, or who have the desire for violence, destruction, and murder. Those who gather there do not seem to be aware that they are actually in hell.

I witnessed these sights and felt the misery amid bloodshed and scorching heat. Helpful words would not provide any sort of relief there. As far as I saw, I could not imagine any angel to possibly come and speak to these spirits and guide them to heaven. Because of the primary reason causing these spirits to be there, it would take some amount of time before their memories faded away. They were those who never listened to what others had to say.

They held desires for destruction and violence; they were filled with hatred and wished to thoroughly crush their opponents. These desires were immensely strong. The fierce desire to utterly destroy the enemy had turned into the heat of the Hell of Scorching Heat. It was so hot while I was there, that it felt as if my right arm would catch fire up to my shoulder and burn off.

Acts of terrorism and war
Create hell in the other world

Considering our afterlife in the spirit world, we must prevent acts of murder, violence, and destruction from spreading in this world on Earth. What I saw during my visit was similar to the areas where acts of terrorism occur in this world. But should a war break out on Earth, an even more massive amount of horrible events would occur, with extremely prolonged aftereffects in the spirit world. It would certainly bring about much greater problems and tragedies. When even acts of terrorism can bring about such horrific situations, it is all the more imperative that a war should be taken very seriously.

War immediately creates a realm in hell*, deeply embedding hatred in the souls of many. It will create karma in people's souls that will be carried out through reincarnations, resulting in them repeating their atonement and revenge for many lifetimes. The experience of a massive trauma in life through destructive acts and murder will have an immense impact on people's souls, and its memories will last for about one to two thousand years.

In the modern day, the development of gunpowder, explosives and other new weaponry has advanced, enabling us to carry out various destructive acts and slaughter from afar without ever having feelings of guilt. In this era, a single push of a button would enable the killing of a massive amount of people, so the feeling of guilt is minimal. As a result of this mass destruction, however, a Hell of Agonizing Cries will be formed just as it did in the past. We must recognize that terrorism and war will create a serious karma on the individual level, as well as for group karma.†

As far as I have observed these tragic scenes in the spirit world, it was impossible even for angels to persuade the spirits there; these horrific situations would probably continue for some time. They will most probably

---

* A realm of hell was formed in the other world when the Gulf War broke out in 1991. For more details, refer to *My Journey through the Spirit World* (New York: IRH Press, 2018).

† Group karma is an inescapable common destiny shared by all people who belong to the same group or age, such as a society, a nation or humanity as a whole.

experience the same scenarios of destruction from acts of terrorism over and over again. People who committed suicide, for example, would repeat their self-destruction again and again on the same spot even after they had become spirits. In the same way, in the underworld I visited, after such destructive acts of murder and terrorism occur, everything returns to a normal state after a while, only to have a similar event happen again. In this way they repeat the same experience again and again. This will continue until a majority of the inhabitants awaken to the spiritual truth and willingly try to receive guidance to lead a truthful way of life.

The Hell of Lust: Imprisoned Women

The second journey into the spirit world

Having returned from my initial visit to the spirit world around 2:00 am, I was struggling to sleep with its lingering memories, when, once again, I was dragged away for a second experience that started at around 3:00 am. This time I appeared in the middle of slightly brighter and more colorful scenery, so I was initially relieved to find myself in an apparently better place. However, I soon found out that it was also part of hell.

The kind of place I had arrived at for my second round was the Realm of Lust, yet a little altered from the traditional one, just like the *Ashura* Hell. The common image of the Realm of Lust in Happy Science films is often portrayed as a Hell of the Bloody Pond where people suffer in a lava-like bath, but that is a slightly outdated image and the current Realm of Lust does not necessarily take that form. The place I visited had nice scenery that initially made me mistakenly feel that I had arrived someplace like the Astral Realm.

There I found a large building of Western design, which had an orange roof and typical windows. It seemed to be the residence of about ten women of different nationalities, including European, Indian, Chinese, and Japanese. They wore colorful clothing and their appearances varied; they were rather good-looking.

Inhabitants held back by an invisible river

Initially I didn't realize I was in hell; I was just struck by the diversity of the women. But as I was observing the place, I soon began to sense something odd. It seemed to me that the women situated there were imprisoned and unable to escape. They were in a relatively nice Western-style building, but it was actually a kind of brothel. I realized that it was a building to confine women who were working as prostitutes, or who would have been called *geisha* in olden times.

Among them was a girl of only seventeen or eighteen years old. She looked Japanese and was wearing white attire. It was not a dress, but rather like the long undergarment of a Japanese kimono. Since the girl still looked innocent, I thought I might at least be able to quietly help her get out of there. So I secretly guided her out of the building.

The building was surrounded by an open field with some flowers, and seemingly, there was nothing else. However, about five to ten meters (15 – 30 feet) from the building, we came up to a river. It was a transparent river, the sort of which can never be found on Earth. It was a flowing river, yet transparent and invisible to the normal human eye. When we tried to cross it, the girl's attire became so heavily drenched that she almost drowned and we were unable to cross through it. So we returned to the building to try another route, which again ended in failure.

Chased by a witch

I then held my arm around the girl to carry her, trying to escape through the roof. As I flew higher, however, the ceiling grew larger and taller, with no way of going through it. And while we were making our escape attempt, others started to notice that I was trying to take the girl away.

Among them was the proprietress, a woman who reminded me of a witch. Her face was somewhat familiar to me. I'm sure she was a sorceress or a witch; her large bulging eyes, long hair, and immensely strong psychic power indicated as such. As a witch, she looked rather like the old mountain hag that appears in Japanese folktales. She looked to be in her fifties. Although she did not look so evil, she had a frightening face with the traits of a witch—large eyes that gave strength to her gaze.

I quickly understood she was the one in charge, or mistress of the house. Then I gradually came to see that this dominating witch was using her magical power, or some kind of psychic power, to imprison the women and prevent them from escaping. The women were bound by her psychic power.

I tried once again to escape through the ceiling, but then another woman with long hair in black Chinese attire came after us. She initially looked like a normal, attractive woman, but when she started chasing after us, her face turned into something horrific as her mouth suddenly widened to her ears with fangs showing out, and her eyes narrowed with a mysterious glitter. The old mountain hag witch and other women chased us down, preventing us from escape. Thus, nobody was allowed to leave, and should anybody try, or if an outsider tries to help one of them escape, they will pull her back again to keep her inside.

Women under spell

I didn't see any men in the place at the time. But it was obvious that the women had to serve as "sex slaves" and were unable to escape. The existence of such a realm in the underworld means there is an equivalent world on Earth in which women are treated as commercial property and unable to flee from sex slavery. This happens not only in Japan, but also around the world.

There reportedly are cases, for instance, in which women are lured from the Philippines or other Southeast Asian countries with the promise of good-paying jobs, such as hostesses in drinking places or dance performers, only to find themselves being forced into the sex trade as security for taking out loans, but with no way of escape. Such illegal practices have been carried out all across the globe. And there is a place in the underworld for these women, who have been held captive in this way and turned into sex slaves, to go after death. In the other world, too, they are confined in a separate place and apparently put under a spell of "no escape." I'm not sure if these women understand that they are actually in hell.

So, there was no escape no matter how hard we tried. Even if I could successfully remove her from the building, an invisible river would block our way out, and we could neither escape through the ceiling nor the windows of the building. This is how we struggled to break out. I tried to speak with this girl of about seventeen, but it was in vain because she just kept silent. A beautiful young woman, she resembled the Japanese actress Miho Kanno. I was able to talk with the other women a little, but not with her because she said nothing at all.

As we made efforts to escape from those chasing us, I was yanked several times by the silver cord attached to the top of my head like a puppet string, which pulled me up high several times like an astronaut bobbing in space. I thus got pulled out of that place and was drawn back to the earthly world. I think I had been taken for my second visit around 3:00 am and was returned at around 4:30 am. After I came back, I was able to continue monitoring the scene by using my spiritual sight, rather than my physical eyes.

I could not help anybody get out of the Hell of Lust, just like in the previous *Ashura* Realm. In order to

What Is a Silver Cord?

Silver cord is a spiritual cord which links the soul and the physical body. For as long as a silver cord is connecting the two together, the body would not die even if the soul leaves the body. People's souls often leave the body during their sleep and visit the spirit world, regardless of whether they possess a psychic power. This is to remind us not to forget our true natures as spiritual beings. Whenever you have a dream that is in full-color, the chances are high that you go to the spirit world. For more details, refer to *My Journey through the Spirit World* (New York: IRH Press, 2018).

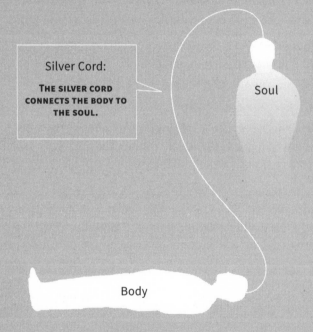

Silver Cord:

THE SILVER CORD CONNECTS THE BODY TO THE SOUL.

Soul

Body

People around the world have known about the silver cord since ancient times. Descriptions of it have been found in the Old Testament as well as in some books from the age of Socrates. Also, in Japan, the silver cord has traditionally been referred to as the "umbilical cord of the soul."

help inhabitants get out of there, we have to study their individual circumstances, how and why they had ended up there, and work out the way for each individual to escape. There are many such "spiritual fields" in the underworld. Angels cannot just go and swiftly help the inhabitants out; these stranded inhabitants are under a kind of magical power or spell, making it impossible for them to leave.

Hell is not all necessarily like a bowl-shaped crater or an inescapable bloody pond. There are also places like the one I've just spoken of. The women there had probably been carried some prisonlike burden while they were alive. For example: one could have had unpaid loans, one could have broken a law and was unable to return to mainstream life, one could have had negative feelings toward one's parents or siblings, or one could have lived under threatening conditions. Even after they died, they have retained such constrictive fears and been unable to free themselves from such bondage. This is an example of how fear and oppression experienced during one's lifetime can strongly constrain the human soul, preventing one from getting free.

An indispensable salvation factor

It sometimes happens that some of the women who are forced into sex trafficking, made to do illegal work, and unable to escape from this underground network, are killed while carrying out their undesirable labor. But it seems these women have not received appropriate guidance in the other world after they have died.

Those who had no knowledge of the truth about the spirit world or spiritual truths while they were alive would have no clue of understanding, upon returning to the spirit world after death and find themselves in such a modern type of hell. They would not realize what exactly has happened to them, why they have found themselves in such a place, and how they could get out of there. Additionally, they would be bound by the spells of a witch-like being who had stronger power than they did. It would be extremely difficult to break through these spells and escape. This is the impression I had.

If, despite the oppressive life of confinement, they had found a single light of salvation and had some connection to the Truth while they were alive by coming across a Happy Science monthly magazine, movie, lecture, or book of Truth, for example, then they would most probably find a way to escape. If the person, even under restriction, had the chance to go out and attend some kind of a gathering at a local temple of Happy Science to make a few Dharma friends or learn the Truth while alive, he or she would certainly get a chance to escape the current underworld. But if they had no knowledge of the Truth, they cannot flee, because a psychological wall would appear in many ways to prevent them from doing so.

I'm not sure how long this situation would continue for them; I assume it would be for quite a long time unless something happens to change the situation. As time passes, some will make attempts to escape, while new arrivals are continuously dragged down.

There are probably many similar kinds of hell other than the one I happened to see. In all these places, the inhabitants are made to believe that there is no other way of life, so they cannot leave there. It is actually what I experienced; we could not even proceed more than five or ten meters from the building because an invisible river would prevent us from going further. The confined women would drown, so were unable to cross it. We could not go out through the ceiling either.

This kind of hell does exist, but it is highly likely that the inhabitants there are not aware that they are actually in hell. They probably just think they have been captured by some kind of powerful mistress. So, "knowing" is immense power. If they know where they truly are, they will begin to desire to leave their confinement. Then we can help them out.

When it is time for a chicken egg to hatch, for example, the chick will peck at the eggshell with its beak from inside the egg. Meanwhile, the hen pecks at the same place from outside the egg. Then the egg breaks and the chick hatches. This is called "simultaneous pecking in and pecking out" in Buddhist terms. In the same way, an effort to save somebody from the outside (outside power) alone is not sufficient for one to be saved; the effort to break out on one's own power (power of the self) is also essential. No matter how hard people outside may try to save somebody, if the person in question does not at least try to leave the situation behind, it is fairly difficult to do so. This is obvious from the fact that the girl I tried to save kept silent and did not say a thing. She was probably unable to understand what was going on.

From this we can say that the spreading of the Truth is extremely important. People do not necessarily need a lot of information. Even a small amount of Truth will do. They just need a clue to find a way out. To that end, we must strive to approach people from all walks of life. This is what I came away with after my second journey to the underworld.

4

The Hell of Hungry Ghosts: Food is Taken Away

My third exploration into the spirit world

With the first ordeal by fire and the second by water, I wanted this experience to be over so I could get some rest because I had to make some important decisions and go to headquarters to hold meetings later on that day. Contrary to my wishes, however, a third trip started around 5:00 am when I was once again pulled into the spirit world.

Looking around this time, I found myself to be in an open space like a soccer field. Around me I saw many people, both adults and children. At first I couldn't figure out where I was, but it seemed to be like a soccer field.

Shortly, a very tall foreign man over 190 centimeters in height (6 feet) came and stood in front of me, blocking my view. He looked Australian. Nearby there was also a youngster, perhaps a fifth or sixth grader in elementary school who looked Japanese. The youngster was holding a slice of toast with something spread on it, perhaps butter or jam. Then the tall man suddenly grabbed away the boy's toast. The child jumped up trying to get it back, but it was in vain; the man was too tall and kept it out of reach.

The man ate the toast the boy wanted to eat.

As this scene played out before my eyes, at first I couldn't recognize what kind of place I had been brought to. As I looked around, I saw other similar situations of children holding some kind of finger food, like sandwiches or hamburgers, or holding a toy or plaything, which were then taken away by large adults. Initially I only had a vague impression that this must be some kind of hell, but I didn't really understand what sort of place it was. In fact, it was the Hell of Hungry Ghosts[*]. Like the previous two scenarios, this was also very different from how the Hell of Hungry Ghosts was usually envisioned.

For the children, as they are about to take the first bite into their food, it is suddenly taken away by a tall adult and held up unreachably high. So they burst into tears. They cannot have what they were just about to eat. They cannot play with their toys because they were taken away just as they were about to play with them. And no matter how hard they tried to retrieve them, they could not because the adults were too tall. This is one type of the Hell of Hungry Ghosts. Here, the normally-used images of ogres are replaced by large men who take things away like food and toys from children.

---

[*] The hungry ghosts are traditionally considered to be the spirits of the dead who suffered from starvation and thirst. They are so thin that they have protruding ribs and bloated bellies.

Children and unaccomplished goals

Since there were a lot of children there, I observed them to see what kind of children they were. The conventional inhabitants of the Hell of Hungry Ghosts are children who died from starvation due to lack of food and suffer as hungry ghosts. But the children I saw this time were different from that situation. Their real problem was not about food. Food was a symbol, representing the desire to acquire something and the feeling of not being able to obtain the thing they wanted.

So I asked the young boy who had his toast taken by the large man in front of me, "Who on earth are you?" The child answered, "I am a student studying for an exam." From his age, I could see the youngster was a student apparently preparing for an entrance exam to a prestigious junior high school. The reason the student suffered was because, although he tried hard to pass the test, he had failed.

This was a new discovery; I had never imagined that children who suffered greatly in preparation for entrance exams would find themselves in the Hell of Hungry Ghosts after they die.[*] It was surprising to see how they would be

---

[*] Even children can be attuned to the spirits in hell and get possessed by them if they are in a bad state of mind. Juvenile delinquents are in fact often under negative spiritual influence by these spirits. Therefore, academic learning alone is not enough in educating children; they also need to learn the religious truths including the existence of souls, heaven and hell, to cultivate their sentiments.

considered hungry ghosts. There are many children in this world who study so hard to successfully gain entrance to a prestigious junior high school, high school or university to meet the expectations of their parents. Among them are some who, despite desperately wanting to pass the exams, commit suicide because of the severe stress or due to the heartbreak of failure, while others may die of unfortunate causes like childhood illnesses. These children, who leave behind some kind of resentment when they die, find themselves in this kind of place.

They are children who passed away without being able to fulfill their parents' hopes and dreams. Many of them, I imagine, have committed suicide in modern times. There are also children who worked to achieve some goal under pressure from their parents and the stress it involved, but died without completing the goal and left behind some resentment. These children are in the Hell of Hungry Ghosts of the modern style. In this place, each child holds a different thing in his or her hand—food, a plaything, or other object of attachment—but they all cry and scream after having the object they crave being taken away from them by a large adult. The location was like a soccer field, which gave me the impression that there were plenty of children. This was the experience I had.

The large Australian man did not look like a typical ogre. I was somehow able to converse with him in English, and I tried to persuade him saying, "Why don't you give back that piece of bread to the child?" But he replied, "What right have you to say that?" So I admonished him stating, "I am a sort of judge. Children must be protected, and I must secure children's rights. That is the child's food, so give it back to the child." However, he did not believe me, replying, "I've never heard of anything like securing rights for children. And I've never heard of any judges who have such a role." I encountered this kind of place in the underworld, and once again I couldn't settle the case.

The Middle Way of Life:
How to Avoid Hell

Lessons from each realm of hell

So, my first experience was with the *Ashura* Hell, or the Hell of Strife, which involved burning heat. The second was the Hell of Lust, slightly different from the conventional one. It was rather like the Hell of Lust under imprisonment. The third was the Hell of Hungry Ghosts, in which today's children's unfulfilled desires, the pain of not getting what they want, and their feelings of starving have been manifested.

In olden times, it was said that children who died young but unable to return to heaven would go to the shores of the River Styx, where they would pile up stones all day long. When their stone towers reached a certain height, ogres would come and smash them down, so the children would have to start all over again. Nowadays, however, this is not always the case. There is a place in which the item each child craves, whether it be food or a toy, is taken away just as they are about to bite into it or play with it. I saw the lost souls of children in such a place in the underworld.

All three of these are located in a relatively shallow part of hell; they are not located so deep. Taking the first one we can say that violence and murder can be a decisive and material factor in creating a hell. In this sense, it teaches that giving warnings against violence and hurting others as in acts of murder and assault, are still religiously important today.

The second one is obviously related to the sex issue between men and women, but on top of that, it implies that it is not right to unjustly restrain, control, or enslave another person whether the person is a man or a woman. In a strong power relationship, putting others under slavish restraint and controlling them, suppressing, threatening, imprisoning, or depriving another's freedom are extremely grave sins, which will form a hell of its own. In this sense, it teaches the importance of protecting the rights of the people involved, as well as their hopes to live freely; that is also part of religion's mission.

The third one implies: "Modern society is highly advanced, where we can obtain different things almost like magic. It is overflowing with material things, abundant in goods and money, and our lives have been made far more convenient than ever before. But even as we believe we can get anything we want, there are still things we cannot have. Since other people's desires have also become inflated, sometimes we cannot get things in the way we want."

Now that we have secured a minimum standard of life, we have all become greedy. We are always seeking better things and competing to achieve a higher position while kicking others down, living under excessive expectations and stress. We need to know that, as a result of this, the conventional hell, in which we cannot get what we want, unfolds in a modern format.

Buddhist basic principles can be applied to solve this issue. Overheated competition includes excessive or illegal business competition, as well as competition among children. It probably involves different factors, including one's ego and a desire to show off. But we need to teach people a "way of living while knowing to be content," a "Middle Way of life," a "righteous way of life," or a "spiritual way of life in which we practice self-reflection and appropriately control our desires." After my experience touring the underworld, I strongly felt this to be a part of our mission.

Mission of religion: Dissolving hell

The conventional realms of hell taught in Buddhism still exist today, but as described in this chapter they now have much different formats. Because of this, if people go to the realm of my first visit, for example, without having this knowledge of the spirit world, and experience an explosion while on a train, they will most probably feel it is a real incident happening at that very moment.

In the same way, it is highly likely that the inhabitants in my second visit also do not realize they are actually in hell. They may at least understand that they have strayed into a strange place, but probably believe they are still living in the physical world, imagining they have been brought to yet another place, just as they had been taken from their native countries, and are imprisoned and bound once again.

Also, those in the third place probably are not aware that they are in the underworld either. It may be difficult for a child to understand that the experience of having a piece of toast taken away just as he is about to eat it on a soccer-field-like place means it is actually hell. It is not so easy to get out of there, either; children also definitely need spiritual knowledge.

So, all the above are accounts of my tour of the three realms in the underworld, though they were located in a relatively shallow area. I experienced the scenes in full color and they felt quite real; I was able to touch, sense the realness, and even feel the vibration of each move. I also felt the heat and cold of the air and even body temperatures. It was certainly different from just a mere dream.

Since the soul is connected to the physical body by a silver cord, when I faced some kind of crisis, as I said earlier, I was pulled from above and bobbed up and down, just like a puppet on a string. This happened several times. It may be similar to diving in water wearing scuba gear, and then be pulled up by a rope. It came with the feeling that I was returning to where I was before. I clearly remember all my experiences. I retain these memories, which were so vivid that I can talk about them as I am now. These are the traits that distinguish exploration into the spirit world from mere dreams.

This experience of visiting three realms in the underworld made me feel that there is still so much to do as a religion. Modern people who go to such newly formed realms of hell after death will probably not be able to recognize that they are in the underworld, nor would they understand how to get out of it. We must continue planting the seeds of Buddha's Truth in the hearts of different sorts of people by teaching about various modern issues. We must carry out this activity powerfully, tenaciously, widely, and without ever stopping. This concludes the story of my exploration into the world of hell.

◆ Self-reflection will lead you up to heaven ◆

I can persuade lost spirits or evil spirits by saying, for example, "This was where you went wrong. Your thinking was wrong in this way, so you should thoroughly reflect on this. You didn't do such and such while you were alive, and instead did these bad things. You said these horrible things to others. You didn't do anything to give back to your parents, teachers, and friends who supported you a lot. You only complained a lot about what others didn't do for you, but did you ever do anything for them?" Listening to such words, they are left speechless.

If we earnestly explain where they went wrong in this way, their faces will eventually lose hardness and their eyes will become gentle; and as their practice of self-reflection advances, their spirit body that was covered in darkness will begin to emit light from the back of their heads. Although the rest of their bodies remain greyish, they will begin to emit light. After this process, the spirits may even start to cry. Humans are not the only ones that cry. As the spirits repent and change their hearts, tears start falling from their eyes; then soot-like dirt that was covering them will begin to wash away, and light will begin to shine forth. If they manage to fully repent from the depths of their hearts, they will be able to rise up to heaven.

It all comes down to the individual's own effort to rise

to heaven from hell. One cannot ascend to heaven without repentance. Relying on external powers alone is not enough. External support may act as the role of a midwife. During birth, it is up to the strength of the baby and the mother's body, but the role of the midwife who supports the process is never futile. Although the baby will eventually be born with or without the midwife's support, the midwife's presence helps to make the process go smoothly. That outside support may be a small amount of help, but this role is not at all wasted.

I have just spoken of saving lost spirits, but I am able to do this because I can actually see spirits and recognize their faults. I can save them to some extent because I possess Dharma power (divine supernatural power), but this would be difficult for common people.

Nevertheless, by studying Buddha's Truth and making efforts to live in accordance with it every day, you will eventually be able to accumulate light within you. It will create a storehouse, storing up wealth. This wealth in the storehouse, namely light, is equivalent to the virtues that you cultivate in this world. We all accumulate virtue by undergoing spiritual training every day, and we are able to offer these virtues to the spirits of our ancestors.

It is similar to having money put aside and being able to offer some of that money to others who are in need and help them. Because you have this invisible mental value called virtue, you can transmit it to others.

Chapter Three

Seeking
the Starting Point
of Enlightenment

Three Checkpoints
To Determine Heaven or Hell

The Starting Point of Enlightenment (1): The Awareness that Humans are Spiritual Beings

Enlightenment is knowing what you are

This final chapter is a simple explanation about the starting point of enlightenment. As it would be unkind of me to say one needs to read all my books to understand how to begin, I am going to describe it in a way that is as easy as possible for new readers of Happy Science writings and even for young people to understand.

What is the most important point? After thoroughly pondering over this question, first of all, I would say that ultimately, enlightenment is all about knowing oneself. It is essential to know the answers to the question: "What exactly am I?"

So, what exactly are you? You usually see yourself as having a physical body so your physical self is no doubt part of what you think you are. In addition to this physical self, there is also your spiritual self, or a spirit body that dwells within your physical body, taking the exact same form as your physical body. You could call it a "spirit," a "spirit body," a "soul," or even a "mind." Whatever you may call it, the unseen mental self that also exists in your physical body gives you a dual structure.

Whether to believe, acknowledge, know, or accept it or not—this is a crucial point in enlightenment. This, in a sense, is an issue that divides humans into two categories.

Buddhism is not a materialistic teaching

Even though Japanese society has progressed with significant scientific advancements, it has regressed on this point. Because materialism, or the study of the physical body and objects, has rapidly advanced, people have focused their attention on the physical aspects of things. With the advancement of technology and progress in scientific fields, there has been a tendency among Japanese people to shy away from speaking of spiritual matters and consider religion old-fashioned.

This may partially be due to the result of Japan's loss in World War II. Even the writings of Japanese university professors of Buddhist or religious studies reflect a tone of embarrassment on the subject of spirits and souls because it sounds superstitious. It is as if they believe interpreting Buddhism in materialist terms is more appealing, when they say things like, "Shakyamuni Buddha taught that human bodies will eventually perish the same way that mud houses will be washed away by the flooding of the Ganges." But their statement is based on a materialistic idea.

It is certainly true that the Buddha used such a metaphor to teach that physical bodies will eventually cease to exist, but Buddhism would not have lasted twenty-five hundred years on such a teaching alone; that mud houses will wash away in a flood is a fact that is obvious to everybody. Even now, there are many houses made of mud in the rural parts of India, where brick houses are a rare luxury. If there was a flood, these houses would certainly be washed away. So, people would naturally find no special meaning in the statement that enlightenment just means understanding that physical bodies will perish just like mud houses being washed away, because it is a mere objective fact. And if the teaching was just about the fact that houses made of reinforced concrete would not be washed away while mud houses would, then it does not deserve to be called "Buddhism"; this is by no means what enlightenment is.

The true meaning behind his words is the idea that no matter how strongly you are attached to your physical body, it will eventually perish, just like the mud house in the flood; it is therefore more important to see the part of you that will not perish as your true self and value it. This is the true teaching of the Buddha.

As the above example shows, the truth is really simple. Nevertheless, eminent authorities, those considered prominent leaders or professors of Buddhist or religious studies, fail to understand this simple truth. Even somebody who is an honorary professor of a Buddhist university says things like, "Everything ends with death. The soul is merely a superstition. Even Shakyamuni Buddha himself refuted it and said that the physical body will perish when it breaks down. Buddhism is based on materialism." This statement signals that Buddhism is facing its end. It is in its final stage if its leaders say things like this.

Christianity also has an aspect that does not acknowledge spiritual matters. This is because those preaching it have become like "regular workers" with no extra thought. True religious leaders cannot help but to sense spiritual things.

Even monks who serve as heads of Buddhist temples say they do not know what happens after death. When asked whether or not the soul exists, or where we will go after death, the reply would just be, "I do not know." They cannot answer people's general questions. There are even those who become defiant and say, "I was taught by my teachers at a Buddhist university and professional training school that there is no soul. I passed my written test answering that everything ends with death. That is the way I graduated from school and received my certificate as a monk." But this is exactly the opposite of the truth. Their understanding has become completely reversed from the truth.

In these circumstances, people would naturally want the true teachings of Buddhism to be taught afresh. Buddhism today has become too extreme and has taken a mistaken path; I cannot allow this situation to go on. We need to put aside the difficult wording of the old, classic scriptures, and explain the true teachings in modern language so that people can easily understand.

Essential requirement for enlightenment

In fact, the starting point of enlightenment is, firstly, being aware that humans are spiritual beings. You can say that people with such awareness have taken the first step toward enlightenment.

If you were to reply to the question, "How much do you believe that humans are spiritual beings?" what would your answer be? Some may say, "I believe more than 50 percent," while others would say, "60 percent," or "80 percent." There may well be somebody who says, "I am 99 percent sure, but I don't know about the remaining one percent; that's what I will discover after I die." The answer differs depending on the individual, but I have fought for over thirty years to prove that it is a hundred percent true. During this time, I have published over 2,500 books (as of May 2019) and given many lectures. People around me have witnessed numerous spiritual phenomena. So there is no room for any doubt for me, as well as for those around me.

This is the most crucial point in attaining enlightenment. If any expert in Buddhist philosophy claims that everything ends with death or that Shakyamuni Buddha's teachings are based on materialism, then, although these words may sound harsh, that person is fraud. My advice to that person would be: "Please be silent. Do not speak, because that way there is still a chance for you to go to heaven. If you keep teaching mistaken ideas, you will have trouble afterward. Teaching false ideas that go against the truth will cause you suffering in the other world."

Let me repeat: Being aware that humans are spiritual beings is of primary importance for enlightenment. You may sometimes sense it as you practice meditation in different ways at Happy Science shojas (facilities for prayer and spiritual training). Some people may occasionally experience some spiritual phenomena, such as seeing a spiritual being or hearing the voice of their guardian spirit.

This point is so crucial that we should never overlook it. No matter how famous a scholar or Buddhist monk may be, if he says, "There is no such thing as a spirit. There is no other world. Everything ends with death," we should never believe it. It is a matter of black or white, like choosing between the front or back of a coin; there is no middle ground. Some scholars and monks argue there is no spirit, based on the tiny portion of the Buddha's teachings that could be interpreted to support materialism, but they were extracted from the vast amount of his teachings and pieced together. There are actually overwhelmingly more parts in Buddhist scriptures that contain passages showing that the Buddha acknowledged the existence of spiritual beings. You can find many such examples in the scriptures.

Shakyamuni Buddha acknowledged the existence of gods, or high spirits as we call them in Happy Science. Buddhist scriptures have descriptions of a large number of gods. They also have descriptions of demons. Scholars and monks often regard demons as just symbols of some mental delusion, and interpret them in that manner to reflect modern thinking. But the descriptions of the demons are actually based on true stories and they did happen as described. I myself have also had similar experiences as Shakyamuni Buddha did. So, the first essential starting point of enlightenment is to be aware that humans are spiritual beings.

2

The Starting Point of Enlightenment (2): The Way You Live Determines Your Destination in the Afterlife

If your mind is in hell now, It is where you will go after death

The second important point on the path to enlightenment is understanding the following truth: "In the same way that heaven and hell exist in the other world, there is a heavenly way and a hellish way of leading one's spiritual life. The state of mind maintained in this world is what determines whether people will go to heaven or hell in the afterlife." This is a very Buddhist way of thinking, which is slightly different from that of Christianity.

The state of mind signifies the stage of enlightenment; what or how one thinks will directly determine where one will go after death. In other words, if your mind is now attuned to hell, it is where you will go after death, whereas if your mind is attuned to heaven, that is your destination. In the same way, if you have a mind of a bodhisattva, you will return to the Bodhisattva Realm.

So, the state of mind you now have while alive indicates where you will go in the afterlife; there is consistency between this world and the other.

Happy Science teaches this by encouraging people to try to achieve happiness that will carry over from this world to the next. That is why we instruct people to always seek the good, or correct way of life. This is the essence of Buddhist theory.

Why people are possessed by evil spirits

In teaching good and evil, stories of devils and various spirits that can be evil, malicious, or vengeful are often mentioned. These beings actually do exist; there are many cases of people who have witnessed or have had experiences with these beings. Although there are relatively few people who declare that they have met or spoken with angels, you will find that many people have had experiences involving bad spirits. Hell has a very similar aspect to the world on Earth, so people who live in a worldly manner are easily connected it because their thoughts are very close to those of spirits in hell.

When I began experiencing various spiritual phenomena and was then able to communicate with spirits, I was stricken by the existence of evil spirits. This was the biggest shock to me. It was hard to believe that these spirits were once humans, but had turned into what they were after death. They suffered in such pitiful conditions; I could only feel deeply sorry for them.

Among them were many who, while alive on Earth, had the appearance of important people of wealth, high educational backgrounds, or social status such as managers or company presidents. After they died, however, they were in such a deep state of suffering that the only thing on their minds was to find any kind of relief. They were in exactly the same situation as one who is drowning in the ocean, seeking rescue. In other words, they could think of nothing but to save themselves, and they would desperately try to possess anybody who happened to be close at hand to save themselves.

For example, the movie *Titanic* (released in 1997 by Paramount Pictures) showed that many passengers slowly died as they swam in the freezing water when the ship sank. Due to the shortage of lifeboats, only about half of the passengers and crew members were able to get on them. Many of the first class passengers were able to escape danger in this way, but they refused to return to help the people thrown into the ocean; only one lifeboat decided to turn around to rescue others. Once it returned, a lot of people would probably try to grab onto the sides, causing the entire lifeboat to capsize and risk the lives of those already on board. That is why the others were afraid and refused to go back.

Those who have fallen to hell after death and have become lost souls are in quite a similar situation. They are only thinking about how to save themselves, and that is why they possess people living on Earth. To use the above metaphor, they possess the people surviving on the lifeboats which then results in the entire boat turning over, leading everybody to drown. Such a thing does happen. This is the reason behind different misfortunes occurring in a family.

Good religions teach how to get out of hell

Around the time I gave the lecture on which this chapter is based, a certain Japanese group that takes the similar form of a religious cult, received administrative punishment from the Ministry of Economy, Trade and Industry. This group extorted money from people by threatening that they would go to hell if they didn't donate to it. There definitely was a problem with the method they used. Nevertheless, stating that heaven and hell exist and that people will suffer if they fall to hell are not lies at all; they are absolute truths. This is the minimum message religions must endorse.

If there was no such place as hell, it would mean that humans would have no sins and there would be no need for them to be saved; any sort of religious activities would be unnecessary. But the truth is, as I said earlier, there are many who are suffering as if drowning in the ocean. If people who believed in materialism or who mocked religion suddenly became spiritual beings upon death and found themselves in the horrible torture of pitch darkness or in fiery flames, or in a place like the Hell of Agonizing Cries, they will think of nothing other than how to save themselves. But since they had no knowledge of religious truths, they would have no idea how to get out of there.

Obviously, those who know correct spiritual truths have already acquired the knowledge to escape the underworld. Therefore, it is important to listen to sermons in places like churches or temples and receive proper guidance while still alive. After death, religious ministers and bereaved families will conduct memorial services or offer prayers, which will also serve as "throwing a rope" to save the deceased.

Religions conduct these kinds of activities of salvation and that is precisely why they are necessary. In the long period of human history, there has never been a time when religion didn't exist. Even in communist and materialistic countries, underground religious activities have always continued to function. The reason religions have endured is that they teach the truths and represent the world of Truth. Beyond any human thought or logic, truth is truth, and fact is fact; it has always been that way since ancient times, and it will never change.

Thus, the important starting point of enlightenment is, first, to be aware that humans are spiritual beings, and second, to know that heaven and hell exist and to know what is good and evil for a soul to live a life on Earth.

The Way to Return to Heaven

Controlling the Three Poisons of the Mind

We must now further explore what is good and what is evil. Some people may be eager to know it and say, "You teach about heaven and hell, but tell me simply how to avoid the underworld and go to heaven. That's all I need to know; I don't need any other teachings. Just give me the short answer." So here are the basic criteria to check whether you will go to heaven or hell. Please read this carefully, because this knowledge alone will enable you to grab onto the lifeboat and be rescued in the event you are drowning. Please study them well.

The checking points that make up one of the central teachings of Buddhism are the Three Poisons of Mind, namely, greed, anger, and ignorance.

Do not be greedy

Greed means excessive desire. It may be hard for you to objectively tell if you are greedy, but you can tell if others are. Observing the words and deeds of another person, you could say with much confidence, "That person is greedy. He has an extremely strong sense of craving for things." It may be hard to tell in case that person hides it well, but you can usually tell whether somebody is greedy or not.

Being greedy means craving for more than one deserves. A greedy person wants more than what is justified, such as more money, status, or reputation. It is very difficult for you to assess if something is undeserved for yourself, but it is easy for others to see. You are able to know what you deserve if you honestly look at yourself or listen to what other people have to say with an open heart, but if you are self-centered, you cannot.

Success methods advertised in society today introduce many different ideas, but many of them actually work to amplify people's greed. Basically, we must be content with the result that is appropriate for us.

There is nothing wrong with reaping the appropriate result that accords with the effort you make, whether it is manifested in your current income, position, status, or in the form of respect of other people. Receiving the proper social approval from your hard work is not greed at all. That is a natural consequence and is a fair result. However, it is considered to be greed if you attempt to enhance your status by using hidden schemes, such as bribery or planning the downfall of others.

Being greedy is one way to go to hell. Maybe using the expression "the royal road" is inappropriate, but it definitely is a well-traveled, broad and easily road. Greed is such a very common problem. Excessive desires will make you a greedy old man or a greedy old woman, leading you to hell in the afterlife.

Holding back anger
And maintaining peace of mind

The second of the Three Poisons of Mind is anger, or having rage. Almost everybody has an experience of losing his or her temper. If left to their instincts, humans can get angry very quickly. Generally, the world seems to be full of people who offend you. You wouldn't get angry if you only received praise from others, but such a case is rare.

That is because people are usually quick to criticize; while it takes effort to praise others, it is easy to disparage, insult, or speak ill of them. This can be done without being taught; negative words come out quickly and easily. So if left to natural instincts, people will often make negative remarks.

Those receiving the negative remarks will then try to protect themselves from what others have said. This desire to defend themselves works instinctively as self-protection, which will in turn cause anger leading them to attack other people. This feeling is somewhat understandable; it is only natural that you would want to return a punch if you received one. However, within this anger lies a kind of animalistic nature, or instinct for self-preservation. It is the action of showing care for oneself. When you are in a rage, you are just reacting like an animal that is trying to protect itself. There is such an aspect to anger.

Look at animals. They are quick to get angry. Dogs get angry quickly, and so do cats. When in a rage, cats attempt to attack a potential aggressor with their tails straight up and their fur bristling. Small as they are, they can nevertheless express anger to scare a dog off and the moment the dog shows a sign of hesitation, the cat swiftly scrambles up a nearby wall to escape. All animals have this aspect to them; they live in constant fear and anger. All animals have the fear of death. They react with anger because they have the fear of becoming prey and being killed at any moment.

Human society can become similar to the animal

world and be filled with anger if it is left to its natural disposition. However, as long as we are born as humans who are expected to make efforts to be closer to God, or Buddha, we need to strive to bring peace to the world, as well as in our minds.

This being so, it is all the more important to hold back anger. We need to pursue serenity within, our peace of mind. We need to know that having peace of mind itself is the state of happiness. This may sound simple but is actually difficult to fully understand.

Somebody whose heart is filled with hatred is not happy. Consider people who hold hatred toward somebody. Would they look happy? I doubt it. The same is true with combatants engaged in wars. Look at the different ethnic groups or countries fighting each other; people in conflict certainly do not look happy. We want to put all our efforts into realizing peace. We must strive to create a world in which all people can co-exist by calmly determining, through discussion, living areas where each can reside, and by acknowledging and accepting each others' differences in character and ideology.

The same can be applied to the individual level. Since people have different characters, it is impossible to make everybody behave the way you would want them to. It is of course necessary to make an effort to guide others in a better direction, but it is wrong to only accept those who follow you and destroy anybody else who does not agree with you. It would be the same as the Holocaust of the Jews during World War II.

There are plenty of people who may not please you or obey you, but you must deal with these people peacefully and try to patiently guide them in a better direction. This requires endurance. You need to be highly persevering in your actions. The same is true with household matters. Most family issues are a matter of tolerance. Endurance and broad-mindedness are necessary.

To maintain peace of mind, it is necessary to cultivate the virtues of endurance, broad-mindedness, and generosity. Control your anger as much as possible and pursue your peace of mind. That is essential. The effort of pursuing a peaceful mind will allow you to attain higher enlightenment. And if everybody has a peaceful mind, the world will naturally become a beautiful place. This is the explanation of anger in the Three Poisons of the Mind.

Overcoming ignorance

Ignorance in the Three Poisons of the Mind means foolishness. To state it bluntly, it is the foolishness of people who have no knowledge of Buddha's Truth[*].

---

[*] Buddha's Truth is the universal Truth that accords with the Will of God, or Buddha. It governs the entire universe.

I'm sure many Happy Science believers seriously study Buddha's Truth. In the eyes of such people who have grasped its essence, it probably seems that there are a lot of people who are conceited without the knowledge of the Truth. In the world there are many people who have become filled with pride and boast that they graduated from elite universities, are elite employees at elite companies, have large incomes or make lots of money, live in big houses, or are landowners. However, those who know the Truth often feel sorry to see these people living in ignorance of the Truth.

This state of not knowing the Truth is called foolishness; this is "ignorance" in the Three Poisons of the Mind. It is sad for one to live a life without the knowledge of the Truth, no matter how important that person may be in this world.

There are many intelligent people in the field of science, for example, astronautical engineers, theoretical physicists, geophysicists, planetary scientists, or computer scientists. Most people, including myself, do not know the workings of a space shuttle. The majority of people have no idea how images are displayed on television either. You could ask employees of electrical appliance manufacturers such as Sony or Panasonic, but even these people might not be able to answer. They may only know about the components they are in charge of and not the overall process of how to produce images.

Such knowledge certainly contributes to the modern development of the world, but it is very sad that people do not know the important Truth that even people in primitive times knew.

A time will certainly come, years or decades later, when you have to pay the price of not knowing the Truth; you will have to make up for any negativity that resulted from living without knowing the Truth. You will definitely be made to experience it for yourself. It will come in the form of an "underworld tour." People create different realms of hell within their hearts and, in most cases, they will experience each one of them. And their study will continue until they graduate from the world of hell.

There are people who are quick to use violence or lie, or even kill other people, for example. In any case, those who had been ignorant of their inner problem will have to face it for themselves and cannot leave the underworld until they fully learn their lessons. This will determine the period of time they need to stay in hell.

Checkpoints for
The Three Poisons of the Mind

Check and see if you have any thoughts or do any of the actions below:

Greed:

☐ The desire for money or a promotion without sufficient effort.

☐ Lying, cheating or tricking others to get money, position, or attract somebody of the opposite sex.

☐ When attaining something desired without putting in any effort, any thought of being unqualified or making more of an effort do not come to mind.

☐ Strong desire to be approved by others and to give a good impression, and becoming upset if not the center of attention.

Anger:

☐ Having a short temper and sometimes uncontrollable rages.

☐ Instant and defensive retorts upon hearing negative criticisms.

☐ Hatred toward a particular person and blaming that person for everything.

☐ Intolerance of a particular shortcoming of a partner.

☐ Scolding a child in an uncontrollable way.

☐ The thought "Others cause my anger, it is their fault that I become angry." No understanding about the importance of making efforts to attain a peaceful state of mind.

Ignorance:
The belief that:

- ☐ Everything will end in death, so people should live in the way they want.
- ☐ Heaven and hell are just superstitions.
- ☐ Happiness depends on money, educational background, and social status.
- ☐ Being a good person is not so important, but those who belong to the elite and economically successful class definitely go to heaven.

* The above checkpoints are just a few examples of wrong thoughts and actions.

Light the Candle in the Minds
Of Every Person Living in Darkness

The act of scolding is justifiable anger

As discussed above, the Three Poisons of the Mind comprised of greed, anger, and ignorance are the criteria to avoid going to hell; if you become able to skillfully control your mind based on a deep understanding of these three elements, you can say you have attained enlightenment, though it is still at a beginner's level.

Let me repeat: First, avoid excessive desires that are beyond the extent you deserve; second, avoid animalistic or unreasonable anger.

There is of course justifiable anger. For example, when a police officer discovers a thief and angrily chases after him it is obviously justifiable. It would be wrong to allow robbery saying, "Thieves are also fellow humans, so they have a right to do whatever they want. Let them just go ahead and rob a bank." This is not right by any means. A doctor reprimanding irresponsible patients is also considered necessary anger. Necessary anger also includes teachers scolding students or children who are misbehaving, and telling them to study with a stern face.

The above cases are not examples of "getting angry," but acts of scolding, which are actually acts of expressing love. These are different. Sometimes scolding is necessary to nurture other people. But in most cases the kind of anger people have is that of rage and are instinctive reactions, so in times like that, try to soothe your anger.

The importance of missionary work

Thirdly, it is important to live in accordance with the Truth. Those without the knowledge of the Truth are living as if groping in the dark. It is like feeling about for candles during a power outage caused by an earthquake, thunderstorm, or hurricane. In the eyes of those who know the Truth, people ignorant of the Truth are in a sad situation in which they are stumbling blindly through life without light.

We can tell these people to light a candle, and hold it up to illuminate the room and look around. This is the act of missionary work. Missionary work is to light a candle within each and every person. This is an extremely important act.

In truth, there are many people who are living in darkness. Although the world seems to be bright and beautiful, many people are actually living in the darkness of ignorance. Over seven billion people now live in the world, yet so many of them are actually groping in the darkness of ignorance, where there is no light. These people are crawling about in darkness, mistakenly believing themselves to be among the highly elite, impressively successful, or having the knowledge to teach others. We need to hand each of these people a candle of light and say, "Put the light within."

Pitiful are those who died without ever knowing the Truth. When you carry out missionary work, you may sometimes encounter people who will not listen to the Truth and simply reject it, like somebody whose body was covered in oil would repel water. There are many such people, but they are only to be pitied. They will not accept any Truth; as if they are covered in full armor, the Truth does not penetrate into their hearts.

In our daily and home lives, however, different kinds of hardship, trouble, disaster, and suffering will inevitably arise. In these moments, we are presented with the chance to awaken to the Truth. Everybody is given these chances; there may be many times where you can look back to see that something that seemed to be a cause of unhappiness in this world was actually an opportunity to find the Truth. For this reason, even if people do not understand the Truth at the time, it is important to wait for the right time and provide them an opportunity.

Sometimes a book of Truth that is offered to somebody will not prove meaning in that person's heart right away, but that person will find understanding in it ten or twenty years later. Even if another person may ridicule what you currently have been doing with a giving heart to help him or her, sometimes that person will awaken to the Truth thirty years later. Some people, believing they had been doing well, will awaken to the religious truth and attain a certain level of enlightenment for the first time when some misfortune such as a bad incident or accident occurs in the family after their children have grown up. Some will awaken even after their death. So, it is extremely important to provide people with an opportunity.

Missionary work is an act of good; be confident that you are doing something good. The world is filled with people who believe that they are looking at beautiful scenery, when in fact it is just an illusion and they are living in darkness. The truth is that this world is only a temporary abode. Thus, the basic level of enlightenment includes the ability to control the Three Poisons of the Mind.

Sincerely wish to help others

Besides these, there are a few more points you need to be mindful about. It is also considered a sin in the spiritual sense to become conceited and puffed up with pride ("Pride"); to doubt or waver in your faith ("Doubt"), and to have various wrongful views ("False Views").* To avoid confusion I will not explain these any further, but basically, as I said earlier, try to fight against the three traits: having desire beyond what you deserve ("Greed"), becoming easily enraged ("Anger"), and having foolishness ("Ignorance"). In doing so, you will be able to take the first step to achieving enlightenment, though it is at the beginning level.

As a result of this, you will be able to have a peaceful mind, thereby increasing your sense of happiness. Those who have increased their sense of happiness will naturally and selflessly want to help others even a little, or contribute to better the world. Sometimes there are people who criticize those who have such a wish, be quick to find fault with them, or claim that they are hypocrites, but please do not be concerned with such criticism; these naysayers just have completely twisted mind.

---

* Buddhism teaches the Six Worldly Delusions which are pride, doubt and false views, in addition to the Three Poisons of the Mind (greed, anger and ignorance).

If you have a sincere wish to help others, it means you are advancing on the path to enlightenment. You can think of yourself as walking the path to heaven right now. This concludes my lecture, "Seeking the Starting Point of Enlightenment."

◆ How to save the spirits in hell ◆

Ancestral memorial services—
A way to save people who have passed away

In Christianity, people often say that one cannot enter heaven without having the belief in Jesus Christ. Some may go so far as to say, unless one converts to Christianity, he or she will be damned to hell. But if what they say were true, it would mean that humankind before the birth of Christ could not have been saved; it would mean that the history before Christ was an age of ignorance, when salvation did not exist.

In Buddhism, on the other hand, there is the concept of ancestral memorial services. This means that Buddhism advocates the saving of souls of people who lived in the past. Since it is rare that souls of those from one or two thousand years ago are still wandering about as lost spirits, ancestral memorial services are held especially for those who have passed away within the last several decades. But still, it works as a way to save the souls of people who did not encounter Buddhism in their lifetimes. Unlike most Christian religions, Buddhism reaches out to save not only people alive today, but also people who have passed away (there is a similar idea in Catholicism, particularly in the intercessory prayer).

However, demons who have been in hell for thousands of years cannot easily be saved. The reason for this is because they have continuously been accumulating evil deeds, and they do so even now. If they stop their sinful deeds, the darkness will diminish and the light will only increase. But since they continue to add on more evil deeds, no matter how hard we try to get rid of the darkness, it never ceases to exist.

Regular souls, on the other hand, will be able to put an end to their wrongful thoughts or deeds by repenting after death, even if they had committed bad deeds during their earthly lives; in this case, their evil will no longer build up. If, instead, they strive to perform virtuous acts in their new environment, their darkness will decrease little by little while their light increases. When the amount of light becomes greater than the darkness within them, they will be able to ascend to heaven. Ancestral memorial services provide such an opportunity to save those who have already passed.

The power of enlightenment is necessary to save spirits in hell

As a prerequisite to conducting ancestral memorial services, you need to undergo spiritual training. First you need to study Buddha's Truth, read books on the Truth, participate in various seminars and activities at Happy Science, deepen your learning, and be able to feel the light of Buddha. As a result of all these efforts, you will be able to transmit some of that light to your ancestors.

It is impossible to illuminate the "night sea" unless you become like a lighthouse yourself that shines a bright beam. A ship may be lost in the night, unable to find its course, but no matter how much you want to save it, you cannot if there is no light in your lighthouse. You must first give out light, rather than just insisting that the ship must somehow be saved, even while groping in the darkness yourself. That is the only way to lead others.

To give out light, people in this world need to study Buddha's Truth and undergo spiritual training. It is no good to conduct ancestral memorial services every day, without making such efforts. You must first practice spiritual discipline and increase the level of your enlightenment. It is through the power of enlightenment that your ancestors can be saved. This is the starting point of ancestral memorial services.

Entrust the high spirits with the salvation of spirits

There is some risk in holding ancestral memorial services, so frequently holding them in the home is not recommended. That is why Happy Science holds the Great Ceremonial Memorial Service for Ancestors, the Perpetual Memorial Service and other services at our Head Temple Shoshinkan. Memorial services are also held twice a year at our branches around the world. It is much safer to conduct them in the presence of a priest. Light from the other participants will also serve to protect you. So it is best to conduct ancestral memorial services at such places.

Furthermore, the guardian or guiding spirits of the participants as well as the angels of light will also be present at our memorial service ceremonies. These spirits can recognize the spirits possessing the homes of their descendants that are causing trouble, and reprimand them, saying, "What are you doing here? It has been you who have caused them trouble all these years." The possessing spirits will then feel ashamed much like children being scolded by their teachers.

If you take part in Happy Science's memorial services, you will be able to have the support from high spirits. When the power of the descendants is not strong enough to save their ancestors, the high spirits will take their place and reprimand the ancestors' spirits who have been doing wrong. High spirits are the most knowledgeable when it comes to spiritual matters, so it is best to entrust them with correcting the mistakes of the lost spirits. This is the quickest way. Attending Happy Science events will provide the spirits of your ancestors with the opportunity to create new relationships with the high spirits in this way. So when it comes to holding memorial services for ancestors it is recommended that you take part in one of the Happy Science ceremonies.

God Embraces Hell with Tears

Right now, beyond this world,
The worlds of heaven and hell do surely exist.
Since times of old,
Hell has been described as a place of anguish,
And heaven as a world of joy.
Indeed, these things are true.
But don't forget,
There is a Being
Who is silently carrying upon His shoulders
The world of hell,
That place of anguish for those who have fallen.

Hell resting on His shoulders, God lets it be;
Which means He accepts their suffering.
Their suffering is not theirs alone;
God feels their anguish just as it were His own.
O, how light and at ease He would feel
If He could let this burden go.
But God has not forsaken the billions of souls
Anguishing now in hell.
Instead, He embraces them.

Because of human foolishness,
Souls who find themselves in hell complain, saying,
"There cannot possibly be
A God or a Buddha in our world.
Society has already given me much pain.
So why must the anguish continue
Even in my death?
If God, or Buddha, were truly love itself,
He would not have let this happen;
There is no sense to this at all.
How unfair this is to me,
To be faced with this dark world of suffering.
Why am I the only one in such anguish?"
However, the truth is
That God accepts these protesting souls;
With eyes full of sorrowful tears,
He embraces them.
Such is the world that these souls live in.
These are the truths
Which we need to come to realize.

God has been shouldering the suffering
And sorrow of all these souls.
But this was neither His original mission,
Nor His original plan.
This world of hell had been formed
As a result of the sins
Humans mistakenly committed.*
But even so,
God has been embracing this world of hell
And has let it rest upon His shoulders.

If, among you,
There are some, by any possibility,
Who, when leaving this world
Years or decades from now,
May find yourselves in the world of darkness,
The world of hell,
Please do not grieve by yourself.
For God will be sharing in your pain;
Please know that
You won't be suffering alone.
No mother is ever glad to see her child
Stumbling and getting hurt;

---

* How the world of hell was created is described in detail in
The Laws of the Sun (New York: IRH Press, 2018).

No father is ever glad to see his child
Falling into a lake.
No parent does not feel pain
Seeing a child injured and bleeding
From an accident.
God feels the same way.

From our own relative human perspective,
The souls in hell may appear to have been
Harmful people.
And so our human nature makes us want to say,
"Those who are now in hell
Were not helpful at all when they were alive;
They were a detriment to us and society.
So they deserve to suffer in hell."
But this is not the way God feels.
God, with shedding tears,
Is trying to pull the children
Out of the lake they have fallen into.
He is holding the bleeding and crying children
In His embrace.
This is who God is.

Once we come to know this merciful love of God
Who is our Parent,
Once we are awakened to this love,
We, His children, cannot but try to help
Those who are suffering.
We must save the hurting children.
When we find children innocently playing
Near the edge of the lake,
Unaware of the risk of falling into deep water,
We must warn them of the danger.

The heart that can never neglect
Somebody's pain and sorrow,
The heart that cannot bear to see others
Suffering trouble and difficulties,
The heart that cannot help
But extend a helping hand,
This is a heart of love.

The heart of love is:
A heart that wishes to save others,
A heart that wishes to help others,
A heart that wishes to be kind to others,
And a heart that cannot turn a blind eye

To the anguish and sorrow of others.
The fact that such a heart dwells in you
Is sole proof that you are a child of God.

I ask you to ponder,
If you were truly made of clay,
Or are a living creature composed of tiny proteins,
Who, over the course of
Hundreds of millions of years,
And a series of coincidences,
Accidently developed into a being
Who can read my books,
Then how is it possible
That a heart of love can dwell within you?

Whether we live in Japan,
The United States,
Africa,
Or Europe—
All people possess the heart of love.
That this heart of love is universal,
Is proof that everybody is a child of God,
That all people are loved by Him.

AFTERWORD

For the past hundred years or so, religion has been replaced by science and medicine and losing its power to save people. The mass media even considers merely talking about the other world or hell as a fraudulent topic.

However, the kind of salvation that newspapers or TV programs can extend is limited to the pursuit of criminals, saving victims in worldly terms, or raising people's living standards in a materialistic way, under the fine-sounding name of social welfare. They even believe that the mind is no more than just the function of the brain or the nervous system, and let this idea prevail unchecked. For them, "life" only means a person's life span in this world.

When the founder and other leaders of the Aum Shinrikyo religious cult were executed, critics and even religious scholars took up whole pages in major newspapers to proclaim arguments like, "This is the matter of an organized crime, and its senior members were inevitably coerced in order to protect their organization," or "All religions harbor insanity." How pitiful it is for them to know nothing about the true fact that good and evil do exist, and so do heaven and hell.

First and foremost, I want you to know the concrete theory of hell explained in this book. Once you have this knowledge, you can work on plans to avoid going there.

Ryuho Okawa
Founder and CEO
Happy Science Group

This book is a compilation of the lectures, with additions, as listed below.

- Introduction -
The Modern Hell: A Possible Outcome for Anyone
Excerpted from the lectures:
Hatten Shikou given on March 24, 1991,
at Kitakyushu City General Gymnasium, Fukuoka, Japan,
and *Shigo no Seikatsu* given on February 5, 2002,
at Happy Science General Headquarters, Tokyo, Japan

- Chapter One -
Introduction to the World of Hell
Japanese title: *Jigokukai Nyumon*
Lecture given on February 19, 2004,
at Happy Science General Headquarters, Tokyo, Japan

- Chapter Two -
An Exploration into the World of Hell
Japanese title: *Jigokukai Tanbou*
Lecture given on November 8, 2006,
at Happy Science General Headquarters, Tokyo, Japan

- Chapter Three -
Seeking the Starting Point of Enlightenment
Japanese title: *Satori no Genten wo Motomete*
Lecture given on April 6, 2008,
at Happy Science Nara Local Temple, Nara, Japan

- Closing Words -
God Embraces Hell with Tears
Excerpted from the lecture:
Yurusu Ai given on April 21, 1991,
at Nagoya Civic General Gymnasium, Nagoya, Japan

- Further Readings on p.128-129 -

Excerpted from the lecture:
Senzo Kuyosai Tokubetsu Gohouwa given on March 12, 1992,
at Happy Science General Headquarters, Tokyo, Japan

- Further Readings on p.160-163 -

Excerpted from the lecture:
Senzo Kuyo no Shinjitsu given on March 5, 1996,
at Happy Science General Headquarters, Tokyo, Japan

ABOUT THE AUTHOR

RYUHO OKAWA was born on July 7th 1956, in Tokushima, Japan. After graduating from the University of Tokyo with a law degree, he joined a Tokyo-based trading house. While working at its New York headquarters, he studied international finance at the Graduate Center of the City University of New York. In 1981, he attained Great Enlightenment and became aware that he is El Cantare with a mission to bring salvation to all of humankind. In 1986 he established Happy Science. It now has members in over 100 countries across the world, with more than 700 local branches and temples as well as 10,000 missionary houses around the world. The total number of lectures has exceeded 2,900 (of more than 130 are in English) and over 2,500 books (of more than 500 are Spiritual Interview Series) have been published, many of which are translated into 31 languages. Many of the books, including *The Laws of the Sun* have become best seller or million seller.

Up to date, Happy Science has produced 17 movies. These projects were all planned by the executive producer, Ryuho Okawa. Recent movie titles are *The Last White Witch* (live-action movie released Feb. 2019), *Hikari au Inochi – Kokoro ni Yorisou 2 –* (literally, "Our Lives Shine Together – Heart to Heart 2 –," documentary to be released Aug. 2019), and *Immortal Hero* (live-action movie to be released Oct. 2019). He has also composed the lyrics and music of over 100 songs, such as theme songs and featured songs of movies. Moreover, he is the Founder of Happy Science University and Happy Science Academy (Junior and Senior High School), Founder and President of the Happiness Realization Party, Founder and Honorary Headmaster of Happy Science Institute of Government and Management, Founder of IRH Press Co., Ltd., and the Chairperson of New Star Production Co., Ltd. and ARI Production Co., Ltd.

WHAT IS EL CANTARE?

El Cantare means "the Light of the Earth," and is the Supreme God of the Earth who has been guiding humankind since the beginning of Genesis. He is whom Jesus called Father, and His branch spirits, such as Buddha and Hermes, have descended to Earth many times and helped to flourish many civilizations. To unite various religions and to integrate various fields of study in order to build a new civilization on Earth, a part of the core consciousness has descended to Earth as Master Ryuho Okawa.

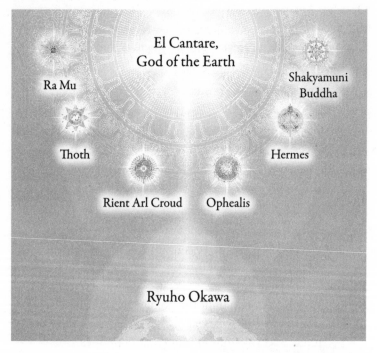

El Cantare, God of the Earth

Ra Mu

Shakyamuni Buddha

Thoth

Hermes

Rient Arl Croud

Ophealis

Ryuho Okawa

Shakyamuni Buddha (Gautama Siddhartha)
Gautama Siddhartha was born as a prince into the Shakya Clan in India around 2,600 years ago. When he was 29 years old, he renounced the world and sought enlightenment. He later attained Great Enlightenment and founded Buddhism.

Hermes
In the Greek mythology, Hermes is thought of as one of the 12 Olympian gods, but the spiritual Truth is that he taught the teachings of love and progress around 4,300 years ago that became the origin of the rise of the Western civilization. He is a hero that truly existed.

Ophealis
Ophealis was born in Greece around 6,500 years ago and was the leader who took an expedition to as far as Egypt. He is the God of miracles, prosperity, and arts, and is known as Osiris in the Egyptian mythology.

Rient Arl Croud
Rient Arl Croud was born as a king of the ancient Incan Empire around 7,000 years ago and taught about the mysteries of the mind. In the heavenly world, he is responsible for the interactions that take place between various planets.

Thoth
Thoth was an almighty leader who built the golden age of the Atlantic civilization around 12,000 years ago. In the Egyptian mythology, he is known as god Thoth.

Ra Mu
Ra Mu was a leader who built the golden age of the civilization of Mu around 17,000 years ago. As a religious leader and a politician, he ruled by uniting religion and politics.

WHAT IS A SPIRITUAL MESSAGE?

We are all spiritual beings living on this earth. The following is the mechanism behind Ryuho Okawa's spiritual messages.

1 You are a spirit
People are born into this world to gain wisdom through various experiences and return to the other world when their lives end. We are all spirits and repeat this cycle in order to refine our souls.

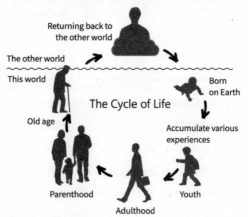

2 You have a guardian spirit
Guardian spirits are those who protect the people living on this earth. Each of us has a guardian spirit that watches over us and guides us from the other world. They are one of our past lives, and are identical in how we think.

3 How spiritual messages work

Since a guardian spirit thinks at the same subconscious level as the person living on earth, Ryuho Okawa can summon the spirit and find out what the person on earth is actually thinking. If the person has already returned to the other world, the spirit can give messages to the people living on earth through Ryuho Okawa.

1 The guardian spirit / spirit in the other world...

2 Goes inside Ryuho Okawa in this world

3 Okawa speaks the words of the guardian spirit / spirit

The spiritual messages of more than 900 sessions have been openly recorded by Ryuho Okawa since 2009, and the majority of these have been published. Spiritual messages from the guardian spirits of living politicians such as U.S. President Trump, Japanese Prime Minister Shinzo Abe and Chinese President Xi Jinping, as well as spiritual messages sent from the Spirit World by Jesus Christ, Muhammad, Thomas Edison, Mother Teresa, Steve Jobs and Nelson Mandela are just a tiny pack of spiritual messages that were published so far.

Domestically, in Japan, these spiritual messages are being read by a wide range of politicians and mass media, and the high-level contents of these books are delivering an impact even more on politics, news and public opinion. In recent years, there have been spiritual messages recorded in English, and English translations are being done on the spiritual messages given in Japanese. These have been published overseas, one after another, and have started to shake the world.

*For more about spiritual messages and a complete list of books, visit **okawabooks.com***

ABOUT HAPPY SCIENCE

Happy Science is a global movement that empowers individuals to find purpose and spiritual happiness and to share that happiness with their families, societies, and the world. With more than twelve million members around the world, Happy Science aims to increase awareness of spiritual truths and expand our capacity for love, compassion, and joy so that together we can create the kind of world we all wish to live in.

Activities at Happy Science are based on the Principles of Happiness (Love, Wisdom, Self-Reflection, and Progress). These principles embrace worldwide philosophies and beliefs, transcending boundaries of culture and religions.

Love teaches us to give ourselves freely without expecting anything in return; it encompasses giving, nurturing, and forgiving.

Wisdom leads us to the insights of spiritual truths, and opens us to the true meaning of life and the will of God (the universe, the highest power, Buddha).

Self-Reflection brings a mindful, nonjudgmental lens to our thoughts and actions to help us find our truest selves—the essence of our souls—and deepen our connection to the highest power. It helps us attain a clean and peaceful mind and leads us to the right life path.

Progress emphasizes the positive, dynamic aspects of our spiritual growth—actions we can take to manifest and spread happiness around the world. It's a path that not only expands our soul growth, but also furthers the collective potential of the world we live in.

PROGRAMS AND EVENTS

The doors of Happy Science are open to all. We offer a variety of programs and events, including self-exploration and self-growth programs, spiritual seminars, meditation and contemplation sessions, study groups, and book events.

Our programs are designed to:
* Deepen your understanding of your purpose and meaning in life
* Improve your relationships and increase your capacity to love unconditionally
* Attain peace of mind, decrease anxiety and stress, and feel positive
* Gain deeper insights and a broader perspective on the world
* Learn how to overcome life's challenges
  ... and much more.

*For more information, visit **happy-science.org***

INTERNATIONAL SEMINARS

Each year, friends from all over the world join our international seminars, held at our faith centers in Japan. Different programs are offered each year and cover a wide variety of topics, including improving relationships, practicing the Eightfold Path to enlightenment, and loving yourself, to name just a few.

HAPPY SCIENCE MONTHLY

Happy Science regularly publishes various magazines for readers around the world. The Happy Science Monthly, which now spans over 300 issues, contains Master Okawa's latest lectures, words of wisdom, stories of remarkable life-changing experiences, world news, and much more to guide members and their friends to a happier life. This is available in many other languages, including Portuguese, Spanish, French, German, Chinese, and Korean. Happy Science Basics, on the other hand, is a 'theme-based' booklet made in an easy-to-read style for those new to Happy Science, which is also ideal to give to friends and family. You can pick up the latest issues from Happy Science, subscribe to have them delivered (see our contacts page) or view them online.*

* Online editions of the *Happy Science Monthly* and
Happy Science Basics can be viewed at:
info.happy-science.org/category/magazines/
For more information, visit __happy-science.org__

CONTACT INFORMATION

Happy Science is a worldwide organization with faith centers around the globe. For a comprehensive list of centers, visit the worldwide directory at *happy-science.org*. The following are some of the many Happy Science locations:

UNITED STATES AND CANADA

New York
79 Franklin St.,
New York, NY 10013
Phone: 212-343-7972
Fax: 212-343-7973
Email: ny@happy-science.org
Website: happyscience-na.org

New Jersey
725 River Rd, #102B,
Edgewater, NJ 07020
Phone: 201-313-0127
Fax: 201-313-0120
Email: nj@happy-science.org
Website: happyscience-na.org

Florida
5208 8thSt., Zephyrhills, FL 33542
Phone: 813-715-0000
Fax: 813-715-0010
Email: florida@happy-science.org
Website: happyscience-na.org

Atlanta
1874 Piedmont Ave. NE, Suite 360-C
Atlanta, GA 30324
Phone: 404-892-7770
Email: atlanta@happy-science.org
Website: happyscience-na.org

San Francisco
525 Clinton St.,
Redwood City, CA 94062
Phone & Fax: 650-363-2777
Email: sf@happy-science.org
Website: happyscience-na.org

Los Angeles
1590 E. Del Mar Blvd.,
Pasadena, CA 91106
Phone: 626-395-7775
Fax: 626-395-7776
Email: la@happy-science.org
Website: happyscience-na.org

Orange County
10231 Slater Ave. #204
Fountain Valley, CA 92708
Phone: 714-745-1140
Email: oc@happy-science.org
Website: happyscience-na.org

San Diego
7841 Balboa Ave., Suite #202
San Diego, CA 92111
Phone: 619-381-7615
Fax: 626-395-7776
E-mail: sandiego@happy-science.org
Website: happyscience-na.org

Hawaii
Phone: 808-591-9772
Fax: 808-591-9776
Email: hi@happy-science.org
Website: happyscience-na.org

Kauai
4504 Kukui Street., Dragon Building
Suite 21, Kapaa, HI 96746
Phone: 808-822-7007
Fax: 808-822-6007
Email: kauai-hi@happy-science.org
Website: happyscience-na.org

Toronto
845 The Queensway
Etobicoke, ON M8Z 1N6 Canada
Phone: 1-416-901-3747
Email: toronto@happy-science.org
Website: happy-science.ca

Vancouver
#212-2609 East 49th Avenue
Vancouver, BC, V5S 1J9, Canada
Phone: 1-604-437-7735
Fax: 1-604-437-7764
Email: vancouver@happy-science.org
Website: happy-science.ca

INTERNATIONAL

Tokyo
1-6-7 Togoshi, Shinagawa
Tokyo, 142-0041 Japan
Phone: 81-3-6384-5770
Fax: 81-3-6384-5776
Email: tokyo@happy-science.org
Website: happy-science.org

Seoul
74, Sadang-ro 27-gil,
Dongjak-gu, Seoul, Korea
Phone: 82-2-3478-8777
Fax: 82-2- 3478-9777
Email: korea@happy-science.org

London
3 Margaret St.
London,W1W 8RE United Kingdom
Phone: 44-20-7323-9255
Fax: 44-20-7323-9344
Email: eu@happy-science.org
Website: happyscience-uk.org

Taipei
No. 89, Lane 155, Dunhua N. Road.,
Songshan District, Taipei City 105,
Taiwan
Phone: 886-2-2719-9377
Fax: 886-2-2719-5570
Email: taiwan@happy-science.org

Sydney
516 Pacific Hwy, Lane Cove North,
NSW 2066, Australia
Phone: 61-2-9411-2877
Fax: 61-2-9411-2822
Email: sydney@happy-science.org
Website: happyscience.org.au

Malaysia
No 22A, Block 2, Jalil Link Jalan
Jalil Jaya 2, Bukit Jalil 57000, Kuala
Lumpur, Malaysia
Phone: 60-3-8998-7877
Fax: 60-3-8998-7977
Email: malaysia@happy-science.org
Website: happyscience.org.my

South Sao Paulo
Rua. Domingos de Morais 1154,
Vila Mariana, Sao Paulo
SP-CEP 04010-100, Brazil
Phone: 55-11-5574-0054
Fax: 55-11-5088-3806
Email: sp_sul@happy-science.org
Website: happyscience.com.br

Nepal
Kathmandu Metropolitan City
Ward No. 15, Ring Road, Kimdol,
Sitapaila Kathmandu, Nepal
Phone: 977-1-427-2931
Email: nepal@happy-science.org

Jundiai
Rua Congo, 447, Jd. Bonfiglioli
Jundiai-CEP, 13207-340, Brazil
Phone: 55-11-4587-5952
Email: jundiai@happy-science.org

Uganda
Plot 877 Rubaga Road, Kampala
P.O. Box 34130, Kampala, Uganda
Phone: 256-79-3238-002
Email: uganda@happy-science.org

ABOUT IRH PRESS USA

IRH Press USA Inc. was founded in 2013 as an affiliated firm of IRH Press Co., Ltd. Based in New York, the press publishes books in various categories including spirituality, religion, and self-improvement and publishes books by Ryuho Okawa, the author of over 100 million books sold worldwide. For more information, visit *okawabooks.com*.

Follow us on:

Facebook: Okawa Books   **Twitter**: Okawa Books

Goodreads: Ryuho Okawa   **Instagram**: OkawaBooks

Pinterest: Okawa Books

RYUHO OKAWA'S LAWS SERIES

The Laws Series is an annual volume of books that are mainly comprised of Ryuho Okawa's lectures on various topics that highlight principles and guidelines for the activities of Happy Science every year. *The Laws of the Sun*, the first publication of the Laws Series, ranked in the annual best-selling list in Japan in 1994. Since then, all of the Laws Series' titles have ranked in the annual best-selling list for more than two decades, setting socio-cultural trends in Japan and around the world.

THE TRILOGY

The first three volumes of the Laws Series, *The Laws of the Sun*, *The Golden Laws*, and *The Nine Dimensions* make a trilogy that completes the basic framework of the teachings of God's Truths. *The Laws of the Sun* discusses the structure of God's Laws, *The Golden Laws* expounds on the doctrine of time, and *The Nine Dimensions* reveals the nature of space.

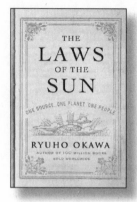

THE LAWS OF THE SUN

One Source, One Planet, One People

Paperback • 288 pages • $15.95
ISBN: 978-1-942125-43-3

In this powerful book, Ryuho Okawa reveals the transcendent nature of consciousness and the secrets of our multidimensional universe and our place in it. By understanding the different stages of love and following the Buddhist Eightfold Path, he believes we can speed up our eternal process of development. *The Laws of the Sun* shows the way to realize true happiness—a happiness that continues from this world through the other.

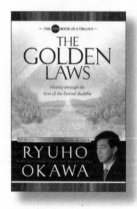

THE GOLDEN LAWS

History through the Eyes of the Eternal Buddha

Paperback • 216 pages • $14.95
ISBN: 978-1-941779-81-1

Throughout history, Great Guiding Spirits of Light have been present on Earth in both the East and the West at crucial points in human history to further our spiritual development. *The Golden Laws* reveals how Divine Plan has been unfolding on Earth, and outlines 5,000 years of the secret history of humankind. Once we understand the true course of history, through past, present and into the future, we cannot help but become aware of the significance of our spiritual mission in the present age.

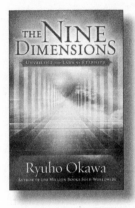

THE NINE DIMENSIONS

Unveiling the Laws of Eternity

Paperback • 168 pages • $15.95
ISBN: 978-0-982698-56-3

This book is a window into the mind of our loving God, who designed this world and the vast, wondrous world of our afterlife as a school with many levels through which our souls learn and grow. When the religions and cultures of the world discover the truth of their common spiritual origin, they will be inspired to accept their differences, come together under faith in God, and build an era of harmony and peaceful progress on Earth.

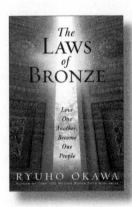

THE LAWS OF BRONZE

Love One Another, Become One People

Paperback • 224 pages • $15.95
ISBN: 978-1-942125-50-1

With the advancement of science and technology leading to longer life-span, many people are seeking out a way to lead a meaningful life with purpose and direction. This book will show people from all walks of life that they can solve their problems in life both on an individual level and on a global scale by finding faith and practicing love. When all of us in this planet discover our common spiritual origin revealed in this book, we can truly love one another and become one people on Earth.

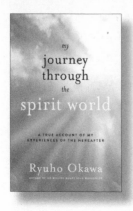

MY JOURNEY THROUGH THE SPIRIT WORLD

A True Account of
My Experiences of the Hereafter

Paperback • 224 pages • $15.95
ISBN: 978-1-942125-41-9

What happens when we die? What is the afterworld like? Do heaven and hell really exist? In this book, Ryuho Okawa shares surprising facts such as that we visit the spirit world during sleep, that souls in the spirit world go to a school to learn about how to use their spiritual power, and that people continue to live in the same lifestyle as they did in this world. This unique and authentic guide to the spirit world will awaken us to the truth of life and death, and show us how we should start living so that we can return to a bright world of heaven.

WORRY-FREE LIVING

Let Go of Stress and Live in Peace and Happiness

Hardcover • 192 pages • $16.95
ISBN: 978-1-942125-51-8

We can cultivate peace of mind and attain inner happiness in life, even as we go through life's array of difficult experiences. The wisdom Ryuho Okawa shares in this book about facing problems in human relationships, financial hardships, and other life's stresses will help you change how you look at and approach life's worries and problems for the better. Let this book be your guide to finding precious meaning in all your life's problems, gaining inner growth no matter what you face, and practicing inner happiness and soul-growth all throughout your life.

THE ART OF INFLUENCE
28 Ways to Win People's Hearts and Bring Positive Change to Your Life

THE CHALLENGE OF THE MIND
An Essential Guide to Buddha's Teachings: Zen, Karma, and Enlightenment

THE STRONG MIND
The Art of Building the Inner Strength to Overcome Life's Difficulties

THE LAWS OF FAITH
One World Beyond Differences

THE LAWS OF MISSION
Essential Truths For Spiritual Awakening in a Secular Age

THE STARTING POINT OF HAPPINESS
An Inspiring Guide to Positive Living with Faith, Love, and Courage

INVINCIBLE THINKING
An Essential Guide for a Lifetime of Growth, Success, and Triumph

HEALING FROM WITHIN
Life-Changing Keys to Calm, Spiritual, and Healthy Living

THE UNHAPPINESS SYNDROME
28 Habits of Unhappy People (and How to Change Them)

THE MIRACLE OF MEDITATION
Opening Your Life to Peace, Joy, and the Power Within

THE ESSENCE OF BUDDHA
The Path to Enlightenment

THINK BIG!
Be Positive and Be Brave to Achieve Your Dreams

INVITATION TO HAPPINESS
7 Inspirations from Your Inner Angel

THE LAWS OF JUSTICE
How We Can Solve World Conflicts and Bring Peace

THE HEART OF WORK
10 Keys to Living Your Calling

MESSAGES FROM HEAVEN
What Jesus, Buddha, Moses, and Muhammad Would Say Today

SECRETS OF THE EVERLASTING TRUTHS
A New Paradigm for Living on Earth

CHANGE YOUR LIFE, CHANGE THE WORLD
A Spiritual Guide to Living Now

*For a complete list of books, visit **okawabooks.com***